CREATIVE BIBLE LESSONS
IN ESSENTIAL THEOLOGY

12 LESSONS TO HELP YOUR STUDENTS KNOW WHAT THEY BELIEVE

PERFECT FOR SUNDAY SCHOOL, YOUTH MEETINGS, SMALL GROUPS, AND MORE!

ANDREW HEDGES

ZONDERVAN®

ZONDERVAN.com/
AUTHORTRACKER
follow your favorite authors

youth specialties

YOUTH SPECIALTIES

Creative Bible Lessons in Essential Theology: 12 Lessons to Help Your Students Know What They Believe
Copyright 2009 by Andrew Hedges

Youth Specialties resources, 300 S. Pierce St., El Cajon, CA 92020 are published by Zondervan, 5300 Patterson Ave. SE, Grand Rapids, MI 49530.

Library of Congress Cataloging-in-Publication Data

Hedges, Andrew A., 1977-
  Creative Bible lessons in essential theology : 12 lessons to help your students know what they believe : perfect for Sunday school, youth meetings, small groups, and more! / Andrew Hedges.
     p. cm.
  ISBN 978-0-310-28326-3 (pbk.)
  1. Theology, Doctrinal—Study and teaching. I. Title.
  BT75.3.H44 2009
  230—dc22   2008048190

Unless otherwise indicated, all Scripture quotations are taken from the *Holy Bible: New International Version®*. NIV®. Copyright 1973, 1978, 1984 by International Bible Society. Used by permission of Zondervan. All rights reserved.

Some of the anecdotal illustrations in this book are true to life and are included with the permission of the persons involved. All other illustrations are composites of real situations, and any resemblance to people living or dead is coincidental.

Web site addresses listed in this book were current at the time of publication. Please contact Youth Specialties via e-mail (YS@YouthSpecialties.com) to report URLs that are no longer operational and replacement URLs if available.

Cover design by SharpSeven Design
Interior design by Mark Novelli, IMAGO-MEDIA, David Conn

Printed in the United States of America

09 10 11 12 13 14 • 20 19 18 17 16 15 14 13 12 11 10 9 8 7 6 5 4 3 2

CONTENTS

DEDICATION

To Anna, Ella, and Abby

May I not simply write and teach these words but live them out so you can come to know the best Daddy of all.

ACKNOWLEDGMENTS

Many thanks to…

The members of the publishing team who contributed to this book—Jay, Dave P., Dan, David C., Amy, Roni, Jody, Marcy, Dave U., Mindi, David W., Janna, and Jen. You made this look good!

The students and translators who attended the basketball outreach of Light of Hope Baptist Church in Minsk, Belarus. Thanks for your help as I learned to communicate these truths more clearly and creatively.

The students at Somerset Hills Baptist Church. Your desire to have fun and learn more about God has inspired me. Thanks for allowing me to be a part of your lives.

Cara, my love. Thanks for always being willing to talk theology with me. You've been one of my greatest teachers. I love you.

PREFACE
THE IMPORTANCE OF THEOLOGY FOR STUDENTS

It's been a long time coming, you know? I mean, we've done a great job of meeting students where they are and learning their points of view. As youth workers, we keep tabs on current cultural trends and prepare to discuss the good and the bad with those under our care. There are several common struggles during the teenage years, and we've been careful to address each issue—dating, suicide, family, friends, media, and the list goes on. Don't get me wrong—I believe we should continue to address these areas. But have you noticed something that connects them all? From where I sit, these are all outward expressions of inward questions about belief. Instead of chasing the expression, what if we began searching the intention? Rather than focus on students' unwise choices, what if we finally became more interested in who students are and what they're thinking and feeling?

This is where theology enters the scene. How we respond to our world stems from our personal views concerning the existence or non-existence of God. Sadly, many students have developed a worldview that's confusing (even to them!) because they don't have a solid understanding of God. At some point everyone begins looking for something or someone to center them and offer them a sense of purpose. As we've kept theology within our seminarian conversations, we've done a great disservice to our students by not allowing them the opportunity to struggle and work through their personal theology.

In "The Purpose of Doctrine: The Search to Know God," Enuma Okoro offers this thought:

> The adolescent years are actually a fertile time to discover and wrestle with doctrinal teachings. When their formative minds are struggling to know what to believe and how to assert their intellectual capabilities, discussing Christian doctrine can be a good way of teaching youth how to "work out their salvation with fear and trembling."[1]

We haven't neglected it entirely. But while we have some great resources for studying biblical theology, albeit in a more hit-and-miss way, we need to be intentional about guiding students in their understanding of the fundamentals of the faith. If students begin wrestling with their God-view, then the typical adolescent issues we've been trying to address could become more Spirit-led decisions, as opposed to being just parent- or God-imposed rules.

In the *Journal of Student Ministries* article "If Everything Is Important, Nothing Is Important: On Teaching Doctrine Effectively," Bodie Weiss wrote, "Since the word *theology* literally means 'the study of God,' logically the first place to begin in developing a doctrine is to begin with understanding God."[2] As you're guided by Scripture, I hope the time you have with your students will take the form of a dialogue—

[1] Enuma Okoro, "The Purpose of Doctrine: The Search to Know God," *The Journal of Student Ministries* 1, no. 3, (September/October 2006).

[2] Bodie Weiss, "If Everything Is Important, Nothing Is Important: On Teaching Doctrine Effectively," *The Journal of Student Ministries* 1, no. 3 (September/October 2006): 48.

probing the possibility and then, prayerfully, the reality of Creator God.

The decision to begin talking theology with your students won't be easy. Charles Swindoll says it well in his book *The Mystery of God's Will*:

> Thinking theologically is a tough thing to do… We much prefer to live in the here-and-now realm, seeing life as others see it, dealing with realities we can touch, analyze, prove, and explain. We are much more comfortable with the tactile, the familiar, the logic shaped by our culture and lived out in our times.

> But God offers a better way to live—one that requires faith, as it lifts us above the drag and grind of our immediate little world, opens new dimensions of thought, and introduces a perspective without human limitations. In order to enter this better way, we must train ourselves to think theologically. Once we've made the switch, our focus turns away from ourselves, removing us from a self-centered realm of existence and opening the door of our minds to a God-centered frame of reference, where all things begin and end with Him.[3]

I believe this is what we all want for our students. But I can't expect my students to care about theology unless they see my passion for getting deeper and deeper into my faith. They need to see me asking hard questions and becoming more amazed by who God is, what he's like, and how he's involved in my personal life. Then God becomes real, and students can begin to consider how real God is to them.

It's difficult for young people to make sense of life or their very purpose for living without first understanding God. In

---

[3] Charles Swindoll, *The Mystery of God's Will* (Nashville: Thomas Nelson, 1999), 17.

his book *Our God Is Awesome*, Tony Evans states, "Knowing who He is defines who we are."[4] To know and understand who we are is important to us all, but it's especially important to teenagers.

This book is designed to provide an organized and targeted beginning to help all students and teachers, regardless of their previous knowledge or learning styles, come to know, understand, and be involved with God the Father. In knowing who God is, may our students truly begin to understand who and *whose* they are. I encourage you to join me in the conversation. We've avoided it long enough, don't you think?

Searching the depths,

Andrew Hedges

[4] Tony Evans, *Our God Is Awesome* (Chicago: Moody Press, 1994), 17.

PHILOSOPHY: LEARNING HOW YOUR STUDENTS LEARN

In order to understand how to most effectively use this book, it's important for you to know the teaching philosophy behind it. In the same way, in order to teach your students effectively, you need to know how they learn. In her book *Learning Styles: Reaching Everyone God Gave You to Teach*, Marlene LeFever provides insight into how people learn. For the purpose of understanding *Essential Theology*, the following paragraphs from LeFever's book will provide a basic understanding of the terms. (Note: The icon that appears next to each description will be used throughout this book to designate activities that fit that particular learning style.)

IMAGINATIVE LEARNER

Imaginative Learners are feeling people who get involved with others and learn best in settings that allow interpersonal relationships to develop. These curious, questioning learners learn by listening and sharing ideas. They see the broad overview or big picture much more easily than the small details. They learn by sensing, feeling, watching. They can see all sides of the issues presented.

ANALYTIC LEARNER

Analytic Learners learn by watching and listening. They expect a teacher to be the primary information giver, while they sit and carefully assess the value of the information presented. These are the students who learn in the way most teachers have traditionally taught, and so they are often considered the best learners. They are strategic planners, and they aim for perfection—the right answers, the As in school and in life. These learners want all the data before they make a decision.

COMMON SENSE LEARNER

Common Sense Learners like to play with ideas to see if they are rational and workable. These students want to test theory in the real world, to apply what has been learned. They love to get the job done. They are hands-on people who, using their own ideas, can analyze problems and solve or fix them. Common Sense Learners, as the name suggests, excel when dealing with what's practical and of immediate importance to them. They learn best when learning is combined with doing.

DYNAMIC LEARNER

Dynamic Learners also enjoy action as part of the learning process, but rather than thinking projects through to their rational conclusion, Dynamic Learners excel in following hunches and sensing new directions and possibilities. These risk takers thrive on situations that call for flexibility and change and find real joy in starting something new or putting their personal stamp of originality on an idea.[5]

God has made each of us in a wonderfully unique way, including the way we learn. These four basic learning styles provide only a glimpse of how students learn during any given lesson. Within each learning style you'll also find students who learn best through various types of activities—**auditory** (hearing) , **visual** (seeing) , or **tactile/kinesthetic** (feeling/doing) . You may have an Imaginative Learner who seems to respond more to pictures or videos. One Common Sense Learner may fit into a more tactile/kinesthetic, or hands-on, style, while another prefers to sit and listen to a tape or guest lecturer. Each student has a different combination by which he learns best.

As you use this curriculum, the best place to start is yourself. Take time to read over the learning styles again, and then consider whether you're more auditory, visual, or tactile/kinesthetic. Which description fits you best? There's no wrong answer. Just keep in mind that most teachers teach the way they learn best. But recognizing your own style will help you

[5] Marlene LeFever, *Learning Styles: Reaching Everyone God Gave You to Teach* (Colorado Springs: David C. Cook, 2002), 20-21, 32.

concentrate on reaching *all* the learning styles found within your group of students.

For your benefit this curriculum has been designed to reach all four learning styles in each session. In the next section, we'll take a look at how you can use this book to reach each student God has given you to teach.

METHODOLOGY: HOW TO USE THIS BOOK

Another goal of this book is to help you teach these truths about God without your students feeling as though they're being taught. Hopefully, you and your students will find this curriculum to hold a much more conversational tone. The idea is to create a sense of dialoguing about who God is throughout each session. In this way students will be led to an understanding of God on their own, as opposed to being told what to believe.

With these things in mind, each of the learning activities is labeled in order to help you see which style and preference is strongest for each activity. However, some of the learning activities may cross over or combine several styles and preferences. The idea is to work out the best scenario for your particular group.

Note that along with the reproducible student worksheets at the end of each session, there are leader-enhanced worksheets that provide you with sample answers and some insight into the issues each question may raise. These aren't designed as comprehensive answer sheets, but as a support for you, the leader, as your group discusses the questions.

Following is a brief explanation of each part of the sessions:

OVERVIEW

Throughout your conversation with the students, we hope these learning objectives are realized.

SETTING THE TONE

Here you'll find a short section with some personal thoughts to help get your mind working through the concepts you'll be discussing with your students.

BREAKING THE ICE

Every conversation needs an icebreaker. The Imaginative Learners will most likely be at the fore of these activities because they get excited about talking things out. You'll get their side of the conversation going right from the start.

TRANSITIONAL TRUTH

These are Scripture-guided insights through which your side of the dialogue will help keep the lesson flowing from one concept to another. You can use these as a framework for how you'll share your heart and thoughts with your students, or you can read it directly from the text.

HEARING THE WORD

These are primarily small-group or pairing activities during which the students will search out God's Word and learn more about who God is and what he does. They'll also allow you to hear how your students are interpreting what they're reading.

SHARING YOUR PERSPECTIVE

These activities will be a great opportunity to get your Common Sense Learners talking about their worldview and how it's changing with an increased understanding of who God is.

MAKING IT PERSONAL

While other parts may appear in a variety of places in each session, we'll always land on a place where students can personalize what they've learned. The Dynamic Learners can run with this segment. It provides an opportunity to show where the theme of the lesson can go after the study time is over and to consider thoughts for further personal reflection.

BRINGING IT TOGETHER

This section will summarize what's been learned, as well as recap the journey to this point. There will be opportunities to review a basic concept from past sessions in order to keep things fresh in the students' minds. Each concept builds upon another, so we can't feel "done" when we've completed the session, but rather one step closer to our understanding of God.

Throughout the book you'll find a number of references to video clips from Highway Video. These are powerful clips for the teenage audience that can be downloaded from the Highway Video Web site (www.highwayvideo.com), but there's a charge to do so. Therefore, you'll need to decide ahead of time if you have the budget to pay for them. (Note: You can also buy a package deal to reduce the price of each individual clip.) If you're unable to download and use these clips at this time, then there's an optional activity included in each session.

One final note about the sessions concerns the timing. The length of the lesson will differ according to the size of your group and the amount of time you decide to dedicate to each part. Generally speaking, the sessions are designed for a one-hour time frame. However, other learning activities can easily be added to fill any additional time. The more time you use, the more opportunities your students will have to learn within their respective learning styles and preferences. The choice is yours!

WHY YOU SHOULDN'T GO TO CHURCH

SESSION ONE

OVERVIEW

This lesson is designed to provide students with a foundation for the knowledge and study of God. Students will discover proofs of the existence of God, understand how they can know God, and increase their belief in the possibility of God.

SETTING THE TONE

Students receive a wealth of information regarding the existence or nonexistence of God. Their friends come from various religious or nonreligious backgrounds. Their teachers share varying views of God in virtually any subject, especially in consideration of science, history, and literature. It's become apparent that the church should be more involved in teaching students what God has revealed about himself in Scripture.

Students desire to learn more about God—in spite of their initial responses. They long for purpose and meaning in their lives, too; yet they also want strong evidence upon which to stand. In these first three sessions, students who may not believe in God may be brought from a place of not knowing to an understanding of how they might begin to know God. This first session is just the beginning of a more logical development of the concept of God and personal faith. The ultimate desire is that students will come away with an understanding that there's only one true and living God (Genesis 1:1; Matthew 4:10) and that they can know him personally.

BREAKING THE ICE
(7-8 MINUTES)

OPTION 1: DOES GOD EXIST?

Begin by saying something like—

> **If there were no God, would you have a reason to come to church? Of course not! Beyond a chance to see friends or a fun experience, church would be pointless if God didn't exist. But how can you know something exists if you can't see it?**

Or grab students' attention from the start by playing the video "Does God Exist?" (You can find this and many other illustrations, including others used throughout this book, at www.highwayvideo.com.)

QUESTIONS TO ASK

1. How do most people feel when they're asked about God? What do they do or say?
→ 2. What are some ways through which people believe they can know about God?

→ **3. How can you know God exists?**

OPTION 2: THE GRAVITY OF THE SITUATION

Begin by saying something like—

> If there were no God, would you have a reason to come to church? Of course not! Beyond a chance to see friends or a fun experience, church would be pointless if God didn't exist. But how can you know something exists if you can't see it?

YOU'LL NEED

• Super Balls, one for each student

At this point hand each student a Super Ball. When everyone has one, tell the students to drop their Super Balls but not to catch them. When the balls settle, ask the students what they observed. They'll probably discuss how the balls kept hitting the ground. Ask them why. The logical response will deal with gravity.

QUESTIONS TO ASK

→ **1. Can you see gravity?**

→ **2. How can you know it exists?** (*Note: Answers will have something to do with seeing the effects of gravity.*)

3. Can we see God?

4. How can we know God exists?

⊀ TRANSITIONAL TRUTH

Though we can't see God with our eyes, we can see the effects and proofs of God's existence all around us. Just as a Super Ball will continue to return to the earth and settle, we should have a similar response to growing in the faith and knowledge of God. God has chosen to reveal himself to us—now the response rests with us. Deuteronomy 4:29 states, "But if from there you seek the LORD your God, you will find him if you look for him with all your heart and with all your soul." For our time together, let's remain open to the possibility of the existence of God.

There are two presupposed truths that we need to accept by faith. This might sound a bit "out there," but think about your life for a moment. You exist. There was a beginning to you—and to all life. There's no way for you to scientifically prove the origin of life because pure science is confined to what one can observe in a controlled setting, including time. Since we can't repeat the experience, we can only create a theory about the origins of life. So regardless of how you think life began, you accept it by faith and probably based upon the information you've seen that would point to the origin.

With that said, let me ask you to suppose two things are true—just as you would with any other scientific theory in order to test it. Both ideas are found in Genesis 1:1—"In the beginning God created the heavens and the earth." In other words, (1) God is, and (2) God acts. The two go hand in hand. We couldn't know God exists if he never acted, especially since we can't see God.

We looked at this at the beginning of the lesson, but let's take a closer look at the proofs of God's existence.

SHARING YOUR PERSPECTIVE
(8-10 MINUTES)

YOU ANSWER YOUR QUESTION

Begin by saying something like—

God's first recorded act—creation—provides a wealth of visible proof of his existence.

Then play "3D Animation of the Human Body" (which is downloadable from YouTube). (Note: This is just one of several pretty cool 3D animations available on that Web site. There are also some extremely eye-opening comments posted about this and the other videos that may help you formulate how you might respond to your students' comments regarding what they see and hear during this session.)

If a video isn't available, consider using a diagram of the human body from a student's health or science textbook or from a similar resource in your local library.

QUESTIONS TO ASK

1. What evidence is there that the world came together by chance?
2. What evidence is there that the world was created by an Architect or Designer?
3. Which theory do you think is more logical? Why?

TRANSITIONAL TRUTH

Psalm 19:1 states, "The heavens declare the glory of God; the skies proclaim the work of his hands." Romans 1:20 follows up on that thought with, "For since the creation of the world God's invisible qualities—his eternal power and divine nature—have been clearly seen, being understood from what has been made, so that people are without excuse." The Bible says creation provides a logical, visible proof of the existence of God.

Just because God exists doesn't necessarily mean we can know God, though. We can know someone built the building we're in right now, but that doesn't mean we'll ever know that individual personally. Job 11:7 states, "Can you fathom the mysteries of God? Can you probe the limits of the Almighty?" We can learn quite a bit about something if we can compare it to something similar. However, Isaiah 40:18 says, "With whom, then, will you compare God? To what image will you liken him?"

How then can we know God?

David, who was called a man after God's own heart, even proclaimed, "Such knowledge is too wonderful for me, too lofty for me to attain" (Psalm 139:6). But don't get up and leave just yet. Remember Deuteronomy 4:29—"But if from there you seek the LORD your God, you will find him if you seek him with all your heart and with all your soul." So let's just consider how we get to know people in everyday life.

HEARING THE WORD
(10-12 MINUTES)

OPTION 1: THE SILENT 20

Begin by asking how we can get to know a person. Answers may include talking with someone, learning about a person from someone else, or observing someone. Then ask which way would be the *best* way. Most will agree that the best way is to get the information straight from the person you're getting to know.

At this point have the students get into pairs, preferably with someone they don't know well. Have them spend five to seven minutes interviewing each other, but have them do so using only gestures and miming. When they're finished, ask the following questions:

QUESTIONS TO ASK

1. What did you learn about the other person?
2. What questions did you ask?

3. **How can you apply the way you learned about your partner to how you might begin to learn about God?**

OPTION 2: STRAIGHT FROM THE SOURCE

Have the students get into smaller groups. Hand each group a copy of the **Straight from the Source** worksheet found at the end of this lesson and give them time to answer the questions. You may want to assign just one or two questions to each group to allow them time to be more thorough in their answers. When most have finished, ask each group to share their answers with the rest of the students.

YOU'LL NEED

- Copies of the **Straight from the Source** handout, one for each smaller group of students
- Pencils
- Bibles

TRANSITIONAL TRUTH

In order to truly know God, we must believe that God really does exist and reveals himself to us. Without this faith, there'd be no need to even attempt to get to know God. If God doesn't exist and act, then church is only a social club or a feel-good activity. But if we accept by faith that he does exist and act—even as we accept the fact that gravity exists—then we can begin our search into the depths of God.

MAKING IT PERSONAL
(5-7 MINUTES)

TWENTY MORE

Say something like—

Just as a game of 20 questions can help us get to know members of the group, we can use a similar idea to get to know God.

YOU'LL NEED

- Index cards
- Pencils
- A hat or other container

At this point pass out index cards and pencils and encourage students to come up with at least one question about God that they'd like to have answered at some point during the rest of the study. Pass around a hat or bowl to collect the questions, and then take time to read them aloud to the group. If possible, let them know when you'll answer their questions. And if some of their questions aren't answered specifically through your study, make sure to take time to research and provide the answers at an appropriate time. Let students know you'll discuss and attempt to answer all of their questions. Remember, it's okay to tell your students you don't know the answer to their great question, but you'll do your best to find the answer and get back to them.

BRINGING IT TOGETHER

Finish things up by saying—

> **As you see who your parents are or how they respond in everyday situations, you may choose to be like them. You may even find yourself acting like them simply as a result of their daily influence on your life. You'll also choose how to deal with those aspects of your parents that you don't like or don't agree with. If we want to know more about ourselves, then we'd be wise to get to know our parents better. And the same thing is true with God. In his book *Our God is Awesome*, Tony Evans states, "Knowing who He is defines who we are." Let's take some time to ask God to guide us and help us as we continue our search.**

SESSION 1:
WHY YOU SHOULDN'T GO TO CHURCH
STRAIGHT FROM THE SOURCE
SMALL-GROUP WORKSHEET

1. If we can't see God, how can we know about him? (John 1:1-18)

2. How can we receive knowledge of God? (Romans 16:25-26)

3. How well can we know God? (1 Corinthians 2:1-16)

4. Who is the Source of information about God? (Ephesians 1:15-23)

5. What's the benefit of knowing God?

SESSION 1:
WHY YOU SHOULDN'T GO TO CHURCH
STRAIGHT FROM THE SOURCE
LEADER'S SMALL-GROUP WORKSHEET

1. If we can't see God, how can we know about him? (John 1:1-18)
   Ultimately, we can only know God if he reveals himself to us. This passage speaks of knowing God through both the Law and through the coming of Jesus.

2. How can we receive knowledge of God? (Romans 16:25-26)
   If they didn't catch it from the details before, this passage tells us we can only know God as he has determined to reveal himself to us. This is the key to knowing God—revelation.

3. How well can we know God? (1 Corinthians 2:1-16)
   While some debate whether we know God "absolutely" or "certainly," the fact remains that we can know God as well as the Holy Spirit opens our minds and hearts to know. We're all sinful and can't expect a clear understanding of the perfect apart from the work and revelation of God through the Holy Spirit, who guides our hearts and minds.

4. Who is the Source of information about God? (Ephesians 1:15-23)
   The key is in verse 17—"I keep asking that the God of our Lord Jesus Christ, the glorious Father, may give you the Spirit of wisdom and revelation, so that you may know him better." All information about God comes from God himself.

5. What's the benefit of knowing God?
   This is open for all sorts of responses. Take note of where your students are and seek to meet them there throughout this study.

IF ACTIONS SPEAK LOUDER...

OVERVIEW

This lesson provides a look at the general revelation of God in his creation. Students will investigate the creation story, understand how it provides evidence of God's existence, and be challenged to be observant of how creation speaks to us of its Creator.

SETTING THE TONE

Students love exploring the big question, "Who am I?" Businesses know this. You can tell from the way they market to teenagers—constantly portraying images of the attractive identities students can take on by owning particular products. Schools know this as well. Science seeks to observe the world around us and come up with some explanation for how it all came to be and who we are in the midst of it.

We have the benefit of God's Word to tell us what happened. Even if your students view the Bible as just another theory at this point, they can at least begin considering the truth found in the creation account in Scripture. As leaders it can be tempting to force the truth on our students. But our responsibility is simply to set the stage using God's Word and allow the Holy Spirit to bring about a personal understanding and faith in each student's heart and mind.

As we consider general revelation in this chapter (specifically, creation), you may find that this only begins to pique the interest of a more in-depth study of God's act of creation. Keep a journal or question box handy for recording the students' questions so you can stay on track with this study and go back to their questions at another time. As you consider exploring theories such as evolution, theistic evolution, and intelligent design, look for good resources to support your study. Considering a number of viewpoints can bring about either a greater understanding *or* some frustrated and confused students. Be sure to gauge your coverage of these areas based upon your students' maturity level and the teachings of your church.

The goal of this session is to expose students to the biblical account of creation and provide an opportunity for students to meditate on how God has shown himself through this world he created.

YOU'LL NEED

• A copy of the movie *I Am Legend* (Warner Bros., 2007) and a way to show it

BREAKING THE ICE
(8-10 MINUTES)

PLEASE TALK TO ME...
Say something like—

In the movie *I Am Legend*, Will Smith plays Robert Neville, a scientist who's trying to save what seems to be left of the human race. After he's just lost his only friend, Robert has to fulfill a promise he made, as well as face the reality of his loneliness.

Play the clip from *I Am Legend*, which can be found by choosing Scene 16 from the DVD menu. The scene begins with, "Please say hello." When the camera cuts away to the street, you can stop the video.

QUESTIONS TO ASK

1. Why does Robert want so much for the mannequin to respond?
2. How is Robert's relationship with the mannequin like many people's relationships with God?
3. When have you ever wished God would just "say hello"?

TRANSITIONAL TRUTH

We all want to hear from God, whether we believe in him or not. It's like there's something built into us that seeks after something greater than ourselves. God knows this, and he's chosen ways to speak to us that we may not immediately recognize. There are two ways in which God has revealed himself to us—general revelation and specific revelation. Today we're talking about general revelation, which is just that—general. It's revelation of a universal aspect of God that's plainly available for all people. For example, we understand God as Creator as we look at his creation. We'll get into this more during our time today.

SHARING YOUR PERSPECTIVE
(8-10 MINUTES)

OPTION 1: TALKING MOUNTAINS

Begin by saying something like, **God's first recorded act—creation—provides a wealth of visible proof of his existence.** Then play the song "Evidence of God" by Geoff Moore & The Distance. To make your opener more visual, create a multimedia presentation of photos set to music that may spark thoughts and reflection upon what we can learn about God from his creation.

QUESTIONS TO ASK

1. **When people view the world around them, how do they think it all came to be?**
2. **Is it possible the world we live in could have happened by chance?**
3. **What evidence do we see around us that someone or something created the world?**

OPTION 2: NATURAL

Show the video "Natural" and then ask your students to share their perspectives.

QUESTIONS TO ASK

1. **When people view the world around them, how do they think it all came to be?**
2. **Is it possible the world we live in could have happened by chance?**
3. **What evidence do we see around us that someone or something created the world?**

YOU'LL NEED

- A copy of "Evidence of God" by Geoff Moore & The Distance (*Home Run*, Forefront, 1995) and a way to play it

YOU'LL NEED

- A copy of the "Natural" video from Highway Video (*Vibe Video Vol. 3*) and a way to show it

TRANSITIONAL TRUTH

As we consider the detail, beauty, and organization of all creation, it makes it difficult to believe that all of this happened by chance. There must be something or Someone greater than us. Psalm 19:1 states, "The heavens declare the glory of God; the skies proclaim the work of his hands." Creation provides a logical, visible proof of the existence of God.

Psalm 94:9 asks, "Does he who fashioned the ear not hear? Does he who formed the eye not see?" In his book *Basic Theology* (Moody, 1999), Charles C. Ryrie puts it this way: "In other words, a living, intelligent creature argues for a living, intelligent Creator." Since we're created beings, we'd do well to examine ourselves to see if we can find evidence of God.

HEARING THE WORD
(8-10 MINUTES)

HEADLINE: MAN HOLDS PROOF GOD EXISTS

Have your students break into pairs or small groups to work on this handout together. Pass out pencils and copies of **Headline: Man Holds Proof God Exists,** found on **page 33.** Allow the students at least five to seven minutes to look over and discuss the sheet together. When they've finished, bring everyone back together for a time of sharing.

> **YOU'LL NEED**
>
> • Copies of the **Headline: Man Holds Proof God Exists** handout, one for each smaller group of students
>
> • Pencils
>
> • Bibles

TRANSITIONAL TRUTH

Man is so special that many try to worship humans or even some other part of God's incredible creation. The apostle Paul tried to keep others from worshipping him even though he'd done some pretty amazing things (by God's power, of course). **In Acts 14:15-18 he said,**

> "Friends, why are you doing this? We too are only human, like you. We are bringing you good news, telling you to turn from these worthless things to the living God, who made heaven and earth and sea and everything in them. In the past, he let all nations go their own way. Yet he has not left himself without testimony: He has shown kindness by giving you rain from heaven and crops in their seasons; he provides you with plenty of food and fills your hearts with joy." Even with these words, they had difficulty keeping the crowd from sacrificing to them.

According to Paul, humans are just further evidence of a Creator who provides for our needs. If people were worthy of being worshipped, then we wouldn't be dependent upon anyone or anything. But we're dependent beings. We need food, air, and water. We need other people. We need...God. And God wants to care for us as God cares for all his creation. We'd do well to remind ourselves daily of how God desires to care for us—if we'd only trust in him.

MAKING IT PERSONAL
(12-15 MINUTES)

BIBLICAL BOTANY 101

Prepare for the planting of seeds by covering with tablecloths, drop cloths, even goggles anything you don't want to get dirty—if your students are particularly out-of-control messy.

Each student should have a flowerpot of his own. I suggest using pots rather than disposable cups because of the length of time your students will be caring for the plants. The plants will be referred to during Session 11. It's nice to have some visuals in your room to help keep the learning moments alive. (Note: Students will need to water their plants each week.)

Give each student a pot and a few seeds. The seed choice is yours, but be sure it's a good annual. For a more biblical touch, you could even try using some mustard seeds. Have the students prepare their pots with the soil and water and then plant their seeds. While you work, you can discuss the following questions:

QUESTIONS TO ASK

1. **What do these seeds need in order to survive?**
2. **What needs to be done on a regular basis to keep caring for these seeds?**
3. **What happens if we don't do anything beyond today?**
4. **So in the end, what has the seed done?**
5. **How is what you do in caring for the seed like what God does?**

As you talk with students, reinforce the idea that God didn't just create us and let us go. Rather, God continues to care for us and be involved in our lives.

BRINGING IT TOGETHER

Finish with something like—

Well, I think we've got a lot to reflect on over the next week. During the last session, we discussed whether we should go to church. Yet we continue exploring who God

is, trusting that God truly does exist and chooses to reveal himself to us. Today, we've looked at how God has chosen to reveal himself through creation. If things still seem a bit abstract at this point, don't worry—we're headed in the right direction. Let's pray that we can come to a greater understanding of God as next time we look at how God has specifically revealed himself to people.

Remember to have students water their plants each time you meet. If you won't be meeting for more than a week, you may need to give the plants an extra watering as well.

SESSION 2:
IF ACTIONS SPEAK LOUDER...
HEADLINE: MAN HOLDS PROOF GOD EXISTS
SMALL-GROUP WORKSHEET

1. How do people, by their own nature, provide proof of God's existence? (Romans 2:14-15)

2. How do humans provide insight into the image of God? (Acts 17:28-29)

3. Read Romans 1:18-32 and answer the following questions:
   - What is it that can be seen by people?

   - Do people have a choice about believing in God? If so, what does this passage say about how people respond?

   - What's the result of a person's choice?

4. Verse 32 shows the extent to which some people choose to turn away from God. Rewrite this verse in your own words.

5. How do you think their minds could be changed?

SESSION 2:
IF ACTIONS SPEAK LOUDER...

HEADLINE: MAN HOLDS PROOF GOD EXISTS
LEADER'S SMALL-GROUP WORKSHEET

1. How do people, by their own nature, provide proof of God's existence? (Romans 2:14-15)
   This may be difficult for your students to come up with, but the main point here is that even without specific knowledge of God, we all follow a law or code of some sort. Since we all search for a standard, we prove that there actually is one common to all humans.

2. How do humans provide insight into the image of God? (Acts 17:28-29)
   Students may say the way we act as "offspring" of God tells us something about God. This is true. Verse 29 also indicates that God is not made up by man but is perfect and beyond what man could imagine or create.

3. Read Romans 1:18-32 and answer the following:
   - What is it that can be seen by people?
     Wrath is first and obvious. But as the passage continues, the idea is that people can see the invisible qualities of God through his revelation, especially in creation.

   - Do people have a choice about believing in God? If so, what does this passage say about how people respond?
     Yes, people do have a choice. The passage says many know about God but choose to turn to themselves and glorify objects of creation rather than the Creator.

   - What's the result of a person's choice?
     God gives people over to their desires—in other words, God lets them live with their choices. God doesn't force anyone to believe in him.

4. Verse 32 shows the extent to which some people choose to turn away from God. Rewrite this verse in your own words.
   This could provide some powerful insight into your students' lives and thinking.

5. How do you think their minds could be changed?
   Possible responses: Miracles, reading Scripture, someone sharing God's story.

THE ALMIGHTY...REVEALED!

OVERVIEW

The purpose of this lesson is to look at how God has chosen to reveal himself through his Word. Students will learn how God has revealed himself by word throughout history, begin to understand how God's revelation comes to us today, and commit to daily search the revelation of God through Scripture.

SETTING THE TONE

What we understand about people can be either clarified or distorted by the medium through which it travels. We consider certain types of technology to be practically perfect in the realm of communication. Then again, I can tell my toddler to take a message to her mommy, but there's no chance my wife will receive the real message—not unless I asked her for a cup of juice.

It's important to our foundation of faith to understand how God chose to reveal himself to the world. Be careful not to gloss over the questions and issues that surround God's revelation—even through his Word. Students who come to faith in Christ need a solid footing when confronted by a friend about who wrote a particular book of the Bible or how we've come to have a copy in our hands. Time is limited in this lesson, but the goal is to expose students to the nature by which God lets people know he's God and he loves them.

This is a huge topic, so you may want to consider taking note of your students' questions and following up during further sessions on why we believe in the Scriptures. Amid the questions, remember to trust the work of the Holy Spirit to do what we can't in bringing about a genuine understanding of God through this and the following sessions.

BREAKING THE ICE
(8-10 MINUTES)

I'M FAMOUS...I THINK

For this activity you'll need to think of some proper names of commonly known people such as Bono, Santa Claus, your pastor, and so on. Write a name on each name tag.

Have the students line up while you stick a name to each of their backs. Tell the students they have about three minutes to go around and ask only yes-or-no questions. Their goal is to guess what the tag on their back says. When a student thinks she has the answer, she should come to you. If she's wrong, then she can keep going. If she's right, she wins. Give her a prize, my friend! (For added humor, play the Casting Crowns song "Who Am I?" while students do this activity.)

When everyone knows the name written on his or her own tag, ask—

- **Was it difficult for you to guess your name? Why or why not?**
- **What was your strategy for identifying who you were?**
- **How do you think this relates to our discussion about God?**

TRANSITIONAL TRUTH

We get to know people every day. Sometimes we meet new people; other times we learn more about the people we already know. Regardless, we ask questions and listen to their responses—these things are central to any relationship. So finding or developing a relationship with God can be done in much the same way.

As we increase our faith in God, we may seek answers to questions about specific aspects of God, but we're still seeing only a small part of the big picture. It can seem like a huge, unfinished puzzle. But the good news is we're not alone. God tells us in 1 Corinthians 2:9-10, "As it is written: 'What no eye has seen, what no ear has heard, and what no mind has conceived—these things God has prepared for those who love him'—for God has revealed them to us by his Spirit. The Spirit searches all things, even the deep things of God." The Holy Spirit can and will guide us as we continue in search of God.

HEARING THE WORD
(10-12 MINUTES)

REVEALING THOUGHTS

Have your students break into pairs or small groups to work on this sheet together. Pass out the **Revealing Thoughts** handout found on **page 42**. Allow the students at least five to seven minutes to look over and discuss the sheet together. When they've finished, bring everyone back together for a time of sharing.

If your students seem interested in learning more about prophecy, a great place to begin understanding God's message through his prophets is the book *Creative Bible Lessons on the Prophets* by Crystal Kirgiss (Zondervan/Youth Specialties, 2002). In it Kirgiss has done a nice job of showing the relevance of Old Testament prophets to our contemporary culture.

TRANSITIONAL TRUTH

Revelation and the Bible are inseparable. The Bible is the completed revelation of God. With the Holy Spirit's guidance, Scripture brings all the pieces together. Even still, God also revealed himself in a beautifully personal way. John 21:25 says, "Jesus did many other things as well. If every one of them were written down, I suppose that even the whole world would not have room for the books that would be written." Studying the life of Jesus Christ is necessary to your coming to find God and know him personally.

SHARING YOUR PERSPECTIVE
(7-8 MINUTES)

YOU'LL NEED

• A copy of the "Chip Ingram: Who Is Jesus?" video, available from Bluefish TV (www.bluefishtv.com), and a way to play it

WHO IS JESUS?

Show the video clip "Chip Ingram: Who Is Jesus?" (Note: Chip Ingram is the president and teaching pastor for Living on the Edge, an international teaching and discipleship ministry.) When the clip is finished, have students discuss some of their thoughts.

QUESTIONS TO ASK

1. What kinds of things have you heard about Jesus outside our group?
2. In John 14:9 Jesus said to Philip, "Anyone who has seen me has seen the Father." If that's the case, then how do you think Jesus relates to our understanding of God?
3. If Jesus weren't real, how would that affect what we're doing here?
4. How can we learn more about who Jesus was during his time on earth?

TRANSITIONAL TRUTH

Scripture is the basis for what we know and understand about Jesus; therefore, it's the basis for what we can know and understand about God. David said, "Your word is a lamp to my feet and a light for my path" (Psalm 119:105). Solomon took seriously the purity of God's revealed Word when he said, "Every word of God is flawless; he is a shield to those who take refuge in him. Do not add to his words, or he will rebuke you and prove you a liar" (Proverbs 30:5-6).

So in order to learn more about Jesus and God the Father, we need to take time to read the great letter God has written to us by the hands of his people—the Bible. As we read, the Holy Spirit can do for us what Jesus asked: "Sanctify them by the truth; your word is truth" (John 17:17).

MAKING IT PERSONAL
(7-8 MINUTES)

THE SENDER HAS REQUESTED A 🅓 ✋ RESPONSE

Begin with something like—

God has revealed himself and his heart toward you. Perhaps you can begin to consider revealing your heart to him.

Give each of the students some sheets of stationery, a pencil, and an envelope. Let them take at least five minutes to write a letter to God. Tell them to jot down a few thoughts about what they know and believe about God. Tell them to include the problems they're having with God or problems they face for believing in God. Tell them to list questions they have about God that they'd like to have answered. If they already believe in God, then they can include what they plan to do with or change in their lives as a result of their belief.

When they've finished, have the students put their letters in the envelopes, seal them, and address the envelopes to themselves before they hand them back to you. You'll be reminded in Session 5 to mail these letters to your students and follow up with them in Session 6 by asking how their questions or opinions have changed along the way.

BRINGING IT TOGETHER

Most of us like to have all our questions answered before we decide to do something. But when it comes to believing in God, there will always be more questions. There comes a point when we have to accept God's existence by faith. We've proposed that God exists, and we've seen evidences of him through observing creation, as well as the written Word of God. Yet God is much deeper. That's why we continue our journey to explore an understanding of God and faith.

As we do, let me remind you of the presence of the Holy Spirit. As we red before, 1 Corinthians 2:9-10 says, "As it is written: 'What no eye has seen, what no ear has heard, and what no human mind has conceived—these things God has prepared for those who love him'—for God has revealed them to us by his Spirit. The Spirit searches all things, even the deep things of God."

We'll learn more about who the Spirit is in a coming session, but just know that God does want a relationship with you. God has made himself known; we just need to respond. Let's ask for the Holy Spirit's help as we continue to reflect upon God and his Word to learn more about what God is like.

SESSION 3:
THE ALMIGHTY...REVEALED!

REVEALING THOUGHTS
SMALL-GROUP WORKSHEET

1. In what two ways has God revealed himself in Genesis 31:11-13 and Ezekiel 1:1, 4-9? What do you think the difference between the two is?

2. What's the difference between God's revelation through the angel in Exodus 3:2 compared with the angel in Luke 2:10-11?

3. How did God choose to reveal himself in Zechariah 1:1 and Romans 16:25-26 and Ephesians 3:4-5? What's the difference between these people and pastors or teachers today?

4. What's the most personal way in which God has revealed himself (John 1:14; Romans 5:8)? How did this tell us more about God?

5. Of all the ways God specifically revealed himself to us, which includes the widest span of revelation?

SESSION 3:
THE ALMIGHTY...REVEALED!

REVEALING THOUGHTS
LEADER'S SMALL-GROUP WORKSHEET

1. In what two ways has God revealed himself in Genesis 31:11-13 and Ezekiel 1:1, 4-9?
   What do you think the difference between the two is?
   *Genesis 31—"angel of God"; Ezekiel 1—vision. One seems to be more physical, while
   the other is visual. While the verses listed here will give your students an idea of the
   difference in visions, they may want to read the rest of Ezekiel 1 for the complete
   description of the vision.*

2. What's the difference between God's revelation through the angel in Exodus 3:2 compared with the angel in Luke 2:10-11?
   *In Exodus 3 the angel of the Lord is a mysterious and elemental revelation through
   the fiery bush, while Luke 2 shows what seems to be a physical being.*

3. How did God choose to reveal himself in Zechariah 1:1 and Romans 16:25-26 and
   Ephesians 3:4-5? What's the difference between these people and pastors or teachers
   today?
   *In Zechariah God spoke through a prophet. The passages in Ephesians and Romans
   speak of the written Word as given through prophets and the apostles. You may want
   to point out to students that this second type of revelation is complete in the Bible.
   People may be inspired to write great things today, but God's direct inspiration of
   the writing of his Word has been completed. Pastors or teachers today can provide
   insight and interpretation, but do not add to the inspired Word of God.*

4. What's the most personal way in which God has revealed himself (John 1:14; Romans
   5:8)? How did this tell us more about God?
   *Both passages refer to Jesus Christ. The students may say that before Jesus came to
   earth, things were more mysterious and abstract. Jesus was God with skin on—someone we can understand and relate to.*

5. Of all the ways God specifically revealed himself to us, which includes the widest
   span of revelation?
   *Possible responses: Scripture, Jesus, creation. The only place we have all things
   recorded for us, though, is in God's Word.*

DESCRIBING THE INVISIBLE
SESSION FOUR

OVERVIEW

The focus of this lesson is to provide students with a basic description of God. Students will learn what God is like, understand how he's a Person and a Spirit, and realize the benefit of God's makeup to every individual.

SETTING THE TONE

If they haven't yet, here's where things can get a bit out of balance. During the next five sessions, you'll be talking through what we can learn about God through his Word. It's important for every person to get to know the God of Scripture, so we study and learn what we can. But hard—even unanswerable—questions are okay. In fact, they're good. We just need to be careful that we don't explain God to the extent that we explain him away. Let me 'splain. No, there's too much. Let me sum up: If a human could understand God completely, then God would cease to be God. We could just put God under a microscope, make a few notes, and move on.

Throughout the next section, keep in mind the transcendence of God. God is a mystery that should be investigated but not necessarily solved. Scripture has given us all we need in order to know God and place our faith in him, but let's not put God in a box and place him in storage. May this be the beginning of a continual awe of who God is and what he means to us.

YOU'LL NEED

- Two clear glass containers of water
- One drop of milk
- A flashlight

BREAKING THE ICE
(5-7 MINUTES)

OPTION 1: ABOVE AND BEYOND

(Note: You'll want to do this first part before your study time begins.) Take two containers of water and place them side by side on a table. Place one small drop of milk in one of the containers. If you shine a flashlight on the container without the milk, you can't see the beam of light. However, when you shine the light on the container with the milk, you can see the beam of light as it reflects on the small milk particles in the water.

Now place both containers in front of your students. Ask them to look at the two containers of water and describe any differences they see. They should look the same. Shine the flashlight on the water-only container and ask them what they see now. Many of them will say they see nothing. Then shine the light on the second container with the drop of milk. Students should see the beam of light inside the glass.

Conclude by comparing this demonstration to being able to see what seems to be invisible by shedding light on the subject. Note: Reinforce the concept of revelation by reminding students we can only know God—who is invisible—if God chooses to let us see the "particles," or reflection, of himself, which is revealed in his Word.

QUESTIONS TO ASK

1. **What can we know about God if he doesn't reveal himself to us?**
2. **How has God revealed himself to us? (Think about the last lesson.)**
3. **How can we now get to know what God is like?**

OPTION 2: INVISIBLE BOY

Begin by saying something like—

> **In the movie *Mystery Men*, Mr. Furious (played by Ben Stiller) and his superhero crew go looking for new recruits to go up against Casanova Frankenstein. So they decide to look up someone who has an interesting power.**

Play the scene from *Mystery Men* (0:36:37 to 0:37:57 on the DVD) where they interview "The Invisible Boy" (played by Kel Mitchell). After the clip finishes, ask your students a few questions:

QUESTIONS TO ASK

1. **How believable is it that something invisible actually exists? Why do you feel that way?**
2. **What would be some benefits to being invisible?**
3. **What would be some drawbacks?**

YOU'LL NEED

• A copy of the movie *Mystery Men* (Universal, 1999) and a way to show it

TRANSITIONAL TRUTH

It can be hard to relate to a God you can't see. It's been a challenge for humans throughout history. That's why so many people have chosen to worship man-made objects, creation, or even other people. However, as we explained last time, God has chosen to reveal himself to us. Now it's our responsibility to take time to get to know God. Jeremiah 29:13 states, "You will seek me and find me when you seek me with all your heart." Let's open our hearts and minds to learn and see more about what God is like.

"'For my thoughts are not your thoughts, neither are your ways my ways,' declares the LORD. 'As the heavens are higher than the earth, so are my ways higher than your ways and my thoughts than your thoughts.'" Even though Isaiah 55:8-9 makes this statement, we can still get to know more about God from his Word. The most difficult part about understanding God is that he's existed since—well, there's never been a time when God *didn't* exist. Moses exclaimed in Psalm 90:1-2, "LORD, you have been our dwelling place throughout all generations. Before the mountains were born or you brought forth the whole world, from everlasting to everlasting you are God."

God is. God always has been. God always will be. God is entirely above and beyond us. And yet, as magnificent as God is, he's taken the time to tell us about himself so we can know God on a personal level. We can know God simultaneously as a Spirit and a Person.

HEARING THE WORD— PART 1
(7-8 MINUTES)

SIMULTANEOUSLY GOD—PART 1

Pass out pencils and the **Simultaneously God** worksheet found on **page 53.** Have the students form groups of four or five to research and answer the top half of the sheet, which relates to God as a Spirit. Take time to go over the students' answers when they've finished.

SHARING YOUR PERSPECTIVE
(9-10 MINUTES)

SKETCHING A PERSON

Give each student a copy of the **Sketching a Person** handout and something to write with. Say something like—

> **Reflect on what you think makes up a person. Whatever you have in your mind, take some time to sketch out a drawing to indicate what things make up a human being. Don't think of just physical attributes, but what makes up the essence of a person. We'll discuss it further when everyone has something down on paper.**

When everyone is finished, have students share their sketches and find the common elements among the drawings.

You'll most likely be able to use their answers to list the three accepted characteristics of a person—intellect, emotion, and will.

QUESTIONS TO ASK

1. **Why would it be important for the intellect, or mind, to be a part of what makes up a human being?**
2. **How does the emotional part of our beings make us unique?**
3. **How is having a will necessary for the makeup of a person?**
4. **How do these things combine to set humans apart from the rest of creation? Or not?**
5. **How does our understanding of a person help us with our understanding of God?**

YOU'LL NEED

- Copies of the **Simultaneously God** worksheet, one for each smaller group of students
- Pencils
- Bibles

HEARING THE WORD— PART 2
(5-7 MINUTES)

SIMULTANEOUSLY GOD—PART 2

Refer back to the **Simultaneously God** worksheet. Have the students return to their groups of four or five to research and answer the questions on the bottom half of the sheet as they relate to God as a Person. Take time to go over the students' answers when they've finished and refer to the students' drawings from the last activity to solidify the points.

TRANSITIONAL TRUTH

As a Spirit and a Person, God is complete in every way. God needs nothing, but he has everything to offer. After Paul stood before an Athenian altar inscribed "TO AN UNKNOWN GOD" (Acts 17:23), he used the opportunity to teach the men of Athens about the one true and complete God: "The God who made the world and everything in it is the Lord of heaven and earth and does not live in temples built by hands. And he is not served by human hands, as if he needed anything. Rather, he himself gives everyone life and breath and everything else" (Acts 17:24-25). The men of Athens didn't need all their gods; they needed only the one true God. Likewise, in God, we have all we need.

MAKING IT PERSONAL
(8-10 MINUTES)

TESTIFY

Say something like—

> Let's try to make this practical. I'm going to read you a couple of statements based on Scripture as well as a couple of questions about how you personally relate to those statements. I encourage anyone who feels comfortable to testify to the truth of these statements in their own lives. Share with us how who you are is impacted by what I've just said about who God is. When you have something to say, stand and testify.

Use the following statements to encourage your students to tell about who God is to them personally:

1. Through Christ you've been brought to fullness in the God who is in control of every power and authority (Colossians 2:9-10). So God as Spirit is over all other spiritual powers. How does that make you feel?

2. You were lovingly created and are intimately known by God (Psalm 139:13-18). The characteristics of God as a Person indicate God has the intellect, emotion, and will to know, love, and take care of his own. What are some specific ways in which this impacts your life?

BRINGING IT TOGETHER

Believing that God exists and desires to have a relationship with us, we can dive deeper into who God is and see how knowing who God is completes us. All we've ever needed is completely met in one Being—God. In order to continue in our learning, we need to follow the instructions implied in Jeremiah 29:13—"You will seek me and find me when you seek me with all your heart." Let's ask God to help us wholeheartedly seek him as we continue our search in the week ahead.

SESSION 4:
DESCRIBING THE INVISIBLE
SIMULTANEOUSLY GOD
SMALL-GROUP WORKSHEET

PART 1: GOD AS SPIRIT

1. When people worship God, how do they relate to him? (John 4:23-24)

2. Where does God live? (Isaiah 66:1)

3. What does God look like? (Luke 24:39; 1 Timothy 1:17)

4. How can we best get a picture of God? (John 1:18)

5. How does God describe himself in Scripture? (Exodus 33:18-23)

PART 2: GOD AS A PERSON

6. How has God exhibited he's a Person in reference to intellect? (Exodus 3:7)

7. How has God exhibited he's a Person in reference to emotion? (1 Kings 11:9-10)

8. How has God exhibited he's a Person in reference to will? (Genesis 3:14-15)

SESSION 4:
DESCRIBING THE INVISIBLE
SIMULTANEOUSLY GOD
LEADER'S SMALL-GROUP WORKSHEET

PART 1: GOD AS SPIRIT

1. When people worship God, how do they relate to him? (John 4:23-24)
   We worship God in spirit and in truth. There's a mystery to it, especially since we aren't relating to God in a physical way. (This doesn't make it any less personal, though!)

2. Where does God live? (Isaiah 66:1)
   It seems like "heaven" is a good response. But it's followed with the fact that no one place could contain God. God is everywhere.

3. What does God look like? (Luke 24:39; 1 Timothy 1:17)
   God isn't human (immortal), is unable to be seen (invisible), and, according to John 14, is a Spirit (without flesh and bone). This is why Jesus' coming to earth was so incredible.

4. How can we best get a picture of God? (John 1:18)
   Through God's one and only Son—Jesus Christ.

5. How does God describe himself in Scripture? (Exodus 33:18-23)
   God says you can't see him and live. When describing himself to Moses, God mentions his "back" and his "face." This is anthropomorphism—a big word your students may have already learned in literature class. It's the act of assigning human characteristics to nonhuman things as part of a description.

PART 2: GOD AS A PERSON

6. We've determined that intellect, emotion, and will are all part of the makeup of a person. How has God shown he's a Person in reference to intellect? (Exodus 3:7)

   This verse shows intellect by describing a logical thought process common to all people: God saw something and logically processed what caused the problem (slave drivers) and then expressed concern about the suffering. (This also shows emotion.)

7. How has God exhibited he's a Person in reference to emotion? (1 Kings 11:9-10)

   Here God shows anger because of Solomon's choice to break God's covenant.

8. How has God exhibited he's a Person in reference to will? (Genesis 3:14-15)

   God determined what he wanted the people to call him.

Note: These three examples are pulled from many instances that show God to have one or more of the three parts that make up a personal being. Be open to sharing and discussing others. These are tough concepts, so remember it's okay to tell students you don't know an answer to a question, but you'll find out from a pastor or spiritual mentor and get back to them. Always be honest!

SESSION 4: DESCRIBING THE INVISIBLE

SKETCHING A PERSON
SMALL-GROUP WORKSHEET

Reflect on what you think makes up a person, then take some time to sketch out a drawing in the boxes below to indicate what things make up a human being. Don't think of just physical attributes, but what makes up the *essence* of a person.

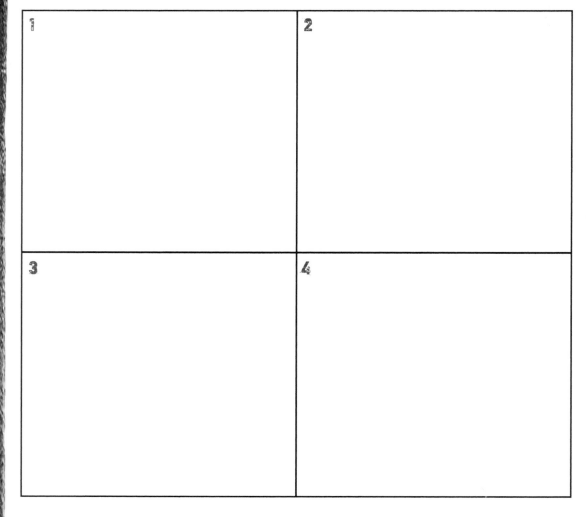

OVERVIEW

The purpose of this lesson is to provide a biblical look at the Trinity. Students will discover each person in the Godhead, understand how they work together in the lives of people, and determine to accept by faith the unity of God.

SETTING THE TONE

The idea of the Trinity is a prime example of why we need to continually remind our students of the mystery of God. Scripture speaks to the Trinity, but a full comprehension of this concept seems impossible. While most people try to teach the details of the Godhead, the purpose here is to present the concept in a "What's in it for me?" way.

The Trinity is necessary for a fullness in God's relationship with every person. As we read God's Word and see how God works all things together for our good, we can rest assured what we learned about in the last session—completion—is possible.

Take some time to look over this session in advance. I've seen the light go on in the minds of many students during the final application of this session (the basketball activity). If you don't have a way to put this in place, begin thinking through a similar scenario to give the students a glimpse of the Trinity. Keep in mind that all explanations come up short when it comes to this truth. Your students may find some faults in your examples, but you can use their questioning as an opportunity to reinforce the greatness and mystery of our God.

YOU'LL NEED

- A shoebox
- Three small mirrors
- A utility knife

BREAKING THE ICE
(7-10 MINUTES)

OPTION 1: REFLECTIONS OF TRUTH

Ahead of time, get an empty shoebox and three small mirrors. Using a utility knife, cut an eyehole in one side of the box. On the opposite side and other end of the box, write the word GOD—backward. Place the mirrors in such a way that you can look through the eyehole and see the word. Mark where the mirrors are with a pencil. Then cut slots with your utility knife so you can slide the mirrors into the box. Finally, you'll want to cut the box lid someplace near where you wrote the word GOD in order to allow light to pass through.

Begin your discussion by saying—

The Bible tells us there are three Persons who are really one God. I know, it's not an easy thing to understand, and

it's not easy to explain it either. But let's try by looking at these mirrors.

Show the students the three mirrors and ask—

Is there anything different about these three mirrors? Can they all do the same thing? What would make anything that one mirror does different from another one? *(The direction it points.)*

The Trinity works like these mirrors. Each Person— God, Jesus, and the Holy Spirit—is equal to the other two in all ways, but functions differently. You see, the Holy Spirit is the One who guides us today. (Slide the first mirror in nearest the eyehole and have a student look into the eyehole.) **Can you see anything?**

Well, let's try including Jesus Christ in the picture because the Spirit reflects Jesus' heart to us. (Slide the second mirror into the middle slot, and have a student look in again.) **Can you see anything yet?**

Okay, let's take the third mirror and let it represent the Father. Jesus said he shared what he saw from the Father. (Slide the third mirror in and give another student a look.) **Can you see anything now? What do you see?** (The word GOD should now be visible and students can see how it takes all three mirrors doing their part to complete the illustration.)

OPTION 2: TRINITY

Show the video "Trinity" and then lead students in a discussion of what they've seen.

QUESTIONS TO ASK

1. **Which Persons of the Trinity are shown in the video?**

YOU'LL NEED

• A copy of the "Trinity" video from Highway Video (*Vibe Video Vol. 15*) and a way to show it

2. In the end the word *God* is shown with the other names rotating around it. What do you think this represents?

3. What do you think about the concept of a Trinity, or Triune God?

TRANSITIONAL TRUTH

God is One. You can't separate him or else you no longer can see him. It's not an easy concept to understand, and I'm not sure we *should* understand it completely. It's part of the mystery and wonder of who God is. From what we read in the Bible, though, God the Father, God the Son (Jesus Christ), and God the Holy Spirit are three equal Persons who each hold a different position to provide a clear representation of who God is. Let's take some time to see where we come up with this concept.

YOU'LL NEED

• Copies of the **A Separate Unity** worksheet, one for each smaller group of students

• Pencils

• Bibles

HEARING THE WORD
(8-10 MINUTES)

A SEPARATE UNITY

Pass out copies of the **A Separate Unity** worksheet found on **page 65**. Have the students form groups of four or five to research and answer the questions together. When most of the groups have finished, have each group share their answers to the questions with the rest of the students.

TRANSITIONAL TRUTH

Each member of the Trinity is equal to the other two as a Person. Their uniqueness comes from the position they hold, yet they're all necessary in order for us to see and understand God. Galatians 4:6 says, "Because you are his sons, God sent the Spirit of his Son into our hearts, the Spirit who calls out, '*Abba*, Father.'" The Father sends the Spirit of his Son to us so we can respond to the Father. Sometimes the best way to make sense of something is to try to work it out in our own words.

SHARING YOUR PERSPECTIVE
(9-10 MINUTES)

YOU'LL NEED

• Optional: A diagram or illustration of the Trinity
• Construction paper
• Markers

TRINITY ILLUSTRATED

If you showed the "Trinity" video at the beginning of the session, remind the students of the way the video illustrated the Trinity. If not, then perhaps you can offer an example of how you'd draw a diagram of the Trinity. (You may find an illustration such as Charles Ryrie's diagram on page 43 of his book *Basic Theology* helpful.)

Once you've shown students a sample illustration, say—

> Now you have a vague idea of how some people would explain the Trinity, but let's see what *you* think. Use the sheets of construction paper and markers to create your own diagram with pictures, labels, and whatever else you can think of. Be prepared to explain your illustration to the rest of the group. We'll discuss your diagrams in a few minutes.

If you have a large group, you can have students work together in smaller groups. Give students time to work out and reteach this concept to each other. This may be where they finally grasp the concept as they work to explain it in their own words.

TRANSITIONAL TRUTH

Knowing **what the Trinity is and** *seeing* **it are totally different. Plus, we can't "see" God or the Holy Spirit. We could have seen Jesus if we'd been alive when he walked the earth, but we can't see him right now. Nevertheless, we can still understand how the three work differently yet together for our good.**

MAKING IT PERSONAL
(10-12 MINUTES)

P-I-G

Set up a basketball hoop of some sort for your group. You can do this activity either outside (or in a gym) with a real basketball hoop and ball or inside with a Nerf hoop and ball.

Say—

> **You've all probably played a game of PIG before, right? The basic idea is that you have to mimic every shot I put through the basketball hoop. So let me have a volunteer.**

Take an easy shot and have the volunteer do the same thing. Then say—

> **Now, that wasn't too hard, was it? But life isn't that way. There are many twists and turns and difficult things to get through. And only God knows the best way for us to get through it all. So the Father tells us what to do.**

At this point give some really crazy directions to your volunteer and tell her to take the shot. It will be hard for her to know what to do because she hasn't seen it done. This works well for our illustration.

After she takes the shot, say—

> **That wasn't quite what I had in mind. Maybe it would help if you had an example to follow. God thought so, too. He sent Jesus to live life and show us how it's done.**

Now you do the crazy maneuvering, thrashing, and whatever else you described to your volunteer and then take a shot. (Just make sure you make it.) As you do, make the moves too complicated to replicate exactly. Then have the same student volunteer try to do the same thing.

Ask—

> **Was that easier? Probably, but it was still tough to copy exactly. Now what would make following the Father's words and the Son's example even more perfect? How about if God sent the Holy Spirit to come and live inside of us so our bodies were under the Spirit's control?**

Ask your volunteer: **How would that help you take the shot?**

Ask your students: **How would that help you live life?**

BRINGING IT TOGETHER

God is a mystery, but he makes sense. Everything about God is complete, so it's no wonder that God can complete us like he does. Next up for debate: Are you in a place where you can hear, see, and live the best life God has planned for you? Let's pray and ask God to guide us as we think about that over the coming week.

Reminder: Mail the letters the students wrote to God during Session 3. You'll be making a reference to them in the next session.

SESSION 5: THREE IN ONE
A SEPARATE UNITY
SMALL-GROUP WORKSHEET

1. Read Genesis 1:26 and Isaiah 6:8 and note the pronouns used. What can you observe about God?

2. List the people mentioned in John 15:26-27. What can you observe about God in this passage?

3. Read through Exodus 3:14, John 1:1-2, and Acts 5:3-4. Make a note of the person of focus in each passage. What's stated about each of these people?

4. According to Deuteronomy 6:4-5, how many gods exist?

5. Look up Matthew 3:16-17, Matthew 28:19-20, and 2 Corinthians 13:14. What can you observe about the way each Person of the Trinity works?

SESSION 5: THREE IN ONE

A SEPARATE UNITY
LEADER'S SMALL-GROUP WORKSHEET

1. Read Genesis 1:26 and Isaiah 6:8 and note the pronouns used. What can you observe about God?
   (1) Us, our, and I; (2) God uses both plural and singular forms in reference to himself.

2. List the people mentioned in John 15:26-27. What can you observe about God in this passage?
   (1) The Advocate/Counselor, or Spirit of truth, (2) the Father, (3) me (Jesus), and (4) you. This passage mentions the three Persons of the Godhead.

3. Read through Exodus 3:14, John 1:1-2, and Acts 5:3-4. Make a note of the person of focus in each passage. What's stated about...these people?
   God is "I AM" and is described as having authority. "The Word" is a reference to Jesus who, according to the passage, "was God." The Holy Spirit is mentioned in reference to someone lying to God. All three are described as God.

4. According to Deuteronomy 6:4-5, how many gods exist?
   "The LORD is one." There is only one God.

5. Look up Matthew 3:16-17, Matthew 28:19-20, and 2 Corinthians 13:14. What can you observe about the way each Person of the Trinity works?   *Jesus is described as an example and as someone with authority to speak. He's also mentioned in regard to grace. The Spirit brings confirmation of Jesus as a dove, is someone whose name should be honored, and is involved in fellowship. The voice is of God the Father, the Director and Authority of all things, who's also the Initiator of love.*

OVERVIEW

This lesson will provide an overview of the natural attributes of God. Students will learn what some of God's natural attributes are, examine how these attributes affect their personal lives and faith, and begin to recognize these attributes throughout Scripture.

SETTING THE TONE

Describing God can be difficult, but God has revealed certain things about himself that offer a glimpse of who he is. Some of these characteristics are said to be natural attributes. For this lesson we'll look at these characteristics that give us an idea of the qualities and capacities of God's nature and essence. For example, you have the ability to learn. The development of our mind is a natural characteristic of every human in some capacity. This will be contrasted with the moral attributes that will be discussed in the next lesson.

God has some awesome natural characteristics, but let's not get too caught up in the "super powers" of God. Some students may see these things and become even more removed from what seems more and more like a fictional being. God is very real, and God's attributes are very real. We can better understand why God has to have these natural attributes as we begin to see how they affect our everyday lives.

The goal is to take students through these descriptions of God in the most "natural" way possible. Before you begin—keep in mind that all of God's attributes are infinite. Let your students know and understand that these descriptions are inconceivably great. King Solomon said in 1 Kings 8:27, "But will God really dwell on earth? The heavens, even the highest heaven, cannot contain you. How much less this temple I have built!" Solomon understood the immeasurability of God, but he also knew God was with him. May our students come to realize that as well.

PRE-SESSION TALK

Take some time to ask your students about the letters they received this week. Ask them where they are with their understanding of God. See if any of their questions have been answered and find out which ones still remain. You can also take this opportunity to ask students if any new questions have come up over the past few weeks. Use your journal or question box from Session 2 to record these new questions so you can be sure to address them at the appropriate time.

BREAKING THE ICE
(7-8 MINUTES)

ON ONE CONDITION...

Say something like—

> **Most of you have probably taken some form of geometry, right? Well, how many of you have ever had to work with "if-then" statements? An if-then statement is just what the name says it is—a statement that proves that "if" something happens, "then" something else will happen. For example, "*If* I go to the mall, *then* I will definitely buy something."** (Or come up with a statement that describes some other thing the students know about you.)

Give each student an index card and something to write with. Say—

> **I want you to create your own if-then statements. Use some information you learned from a previous lesson about God the Father and show a personal application as a result. For example, "If God created the whole world, then I should respect and care for his creation."**

Give the students two to three minutes to come up with something and then ask everyone to share their thoughts with the rest of the group.

YOU'LL NEED

• Index cards (blank), one for each student

• Pencils

TRANSITIONAL TRUTH

We're going to talk about the natural characteristics of God. When we talk about "natural," we're speaking of things that explain the qualities and capacities of God's nature and essence. For instance, you're confined to one space—your body. That's a natural characteristic. But nothing can contain God.

Solomon reflected on this when he was commissioned to build a temple to God: "The temple I am going to build will be great, because our God is greater than all other gods. But who is able to build a temple for him, since the heavens, even the highest heavens, cannot contain him? Who then am I to build a temple for him, except as a place to burn sacrifices before him?" (2 Chronicles 2:5-6). This natural attribute of God, in reference to God's physical ability, is called "omnipresence." God can be everywhere at once. Let's take some time to focus in on some other natural characteristics of God.

SHARING YOUR PERSPECTIVE
(10-12 MINUTES)

THE BEAUTY OF NATURAL

Say something like—

> Let's see what natural characteristics you can come up with when it comes to people. Use the magazines, posterboard, scissors, and glue to make a collage of various things that represent natural human attributes.

When most of you have finished, we'll come back together to see what you've created.

QUESTIONS TO ASK

1. What are some of the more physical things you found? How do those relate to what you know about God?
2. What are some of the abilities you found? How do those relate to what you know about God? *(Note: We're really focusing on potential to act here. The moral attributes will focus on the will to act based upon a standard. So the ability to love could be considered a natural attribute, but it will be more closely linked to the moral attributes as it's an extension of God's will.)*
3. What are some things about God that you just can't find in a picture?

TRANSITIONAL TRUTH

We've talked about God being transcendent—we can't see or understand God unless he exists and reveals himself to us. We've learned that God is both a Spirit and a Person, which is pretty difficult to understand. We've also discussed the three Persons of the Trinity, which is even more difficult to understand. God is definitely transcendent—completely beyond us and our human comprehension. However, God is also immanent—able to be with us.

The apostle Paul says in Ephesians 4:4-6, "There is one body and one Spirit, just as you were called to one hope when you were called; one Lord, one faith, one baptism; one God and Father of all, who is over all and through all and in all." God is here, and God wants to work in and through us. Why? Because God wants us to be full and complete.

HEARING THE WORD
(8-10 MINUTES)

A NATURAL SEARCH

Pass out copies of the **A Natural Search** worksheet found on **page 75.** Have the students form groups of four or five to look up each passage and learn about a natural attribute of God. When they've finished, they'll be creating an "if-then" statement regarding each of the natural attributes they've found and how it relates to their lives. When the groups are done, bring them back together for a time of sharing—but have them share only the attributes of God. We'll save the "then" parts for later.

TRANSITIONAL TRUTH

You've probably heard or even asked the "rock question" before. You know—"Can God make a rock so big he can't lift it?" Well, what do you think? *(Give the students some time to respond.)* We could answer this question in a practical way. Since God's attributes are practical in our lives, let's apply that line of thinking to the rock question. Why would God make a rock so big he couldn't lift it? Would that better our understanding of him? I think the correct answer to the rock question is God wouldn't. God doesn't need to prove himself to us, but God leaves evidence of himself all around us and in his Word. When we think about who and what God is, we can know that God would never do anything that would contradict or go against his character.

Here's an example: God *can* do anything (natural attribute), but God *will* not (moral choice—next lesson) or, in a sense, *cannot* lie (Titus 1:2). Lying would go against the very character of God. Plus, how would lying affect us? If God did that or anything else—good or evil—we'd want to know how it would affect us, right?

MAKING IT PERSONAL
(8-10 MINUTES)

WHAT'S IN IT FOR ME?

Say something like—

> Take a look at your worksheets again. We've already shared what some of God's natural attributes are, but what does that mean to us? Let's share our if-then statements from the handouts.

Take some time to let the students talk out what God's characteristics could mean for them personally. Affirm every response, as this will be the way they truly feel about it. Keep a listening ear and don't spend time correcting things. You won't be able to correct an opinion. Use this as a time to let your students know you care about their thoughts. You'll be able to finish with a thought of your own when the discussion is coming to a close.

BRINGING IT TOGETHER

Here's one final "if-then" statement. If we live in the knowledge of who God is, then our lives can be lived in safety, security, and peace. No, it doesn't mean life will be perfect. But deep down we can feel a sense of safety in the midst of dangerous times because God is everywhere and God is all-powerful. We can feel secure in the fact that God is never-changing and will never leave us. We can be at peace knowing that God knows everything—good and bad—and still wants to be with us. With this knowledge of who God is, life only seems to make sense with God in it. Let's take time to thank God for his presence and to ask for his continued guidance.

SESSION 6: NATURALLY SPEAKING
A NATURAL SEARCH
SMALL-GROUP WORKSHEET

Come up with a term for and definition of the characteristic of God that you observe in the following passages. Then create an "if-then" statement to apply these truths to your personal life. *Example: If God is loving, then I know God will love and care for me.*

1. According to Exodus 3:14 and Psalm 90:2, God is…

   "If-then" →

2. According to Malachi 3:6 and James 1:17, God is…

   "If-then" →

3. According to Psalm 139:1-2 and 1 John 3:20, God is…

   "If-then" →

4. According to Psalm 139:7-10 and Isaiah 41:10, God is…

   "If-then" →

5. According to Job 42:1-2 and 2 Corinthians 6:18, God is…

   "If-then" →

SESSION 6: NATURALLY SPEAKING
A NATURAL SEARCH
LEADER'S SMALL-GROUP WORKSHEET

Come up with a term and definition of the characteristic of God that you observe in the following passages. Then create an "if-then" statement to apply these truths to your personal life. *Example: If God is loving, then I know God will love and care for me.*

1. According to Exodus 3:14 and Psalm 90:2, God is…*everlasting.*

   "If-then" → *If God is eternal, then I know God will always be there for me.*

2. According to Malachi 3:6 and James 1:17, God is…*unchanging.*

   "If-then" → *If God never changes, then I know I can always trust God.*

3. According to Psalm 139:1-2 and 1 John 3:20, God is…*all-knowing.*

   "If-then" → *If God knows everything, then I know God understands what I'm going through.*

4. According to Psalm 139:7-10 and Isaiah 41:10, God is…*everywhere.*

   "If-then" → *If God is everywhere, then I can't be any place without God standing right beside me.*

5. According to Job 42:1-2 and 2 Corinthians 6:18, God is…*all-powerful.*

   "If-then" → *If God can do all things, then I know God can take care of me.*

OVERVIEW

This lesson is designed to provide students with an overview of the moral attributes of God. Students will explore some of the characteristics that make up what God chooses, understand how these attributes can be summarized by God's love, and determine to live in a way that reflects that love.

SETTING THE TONE

This session continues the study of how God describes himself by taking a look at some of God's moral attributes. For this lesson we'll define *moral characteristics* as being those things God chooses to do or a permanent state of the will. That said, you also need to keep in mind that God's moral attributes aren't just things God *does*, but they're actually things that define who God *is*. For instance, God is just; therefore, God will respond in a perfectly just way. This is something we can see or experience. It's hard to experience God's omnipresence (natural attribute) unless he meets us with his love (moral attribute). And that's really the focal point of this lesson—God's love.

Love seems to speak to the totality of God's character. The more I've studied God's Word and searched the depth of God's character, the more I've come to understand what John meant when he said, "God *is* love" (1 John 4:8, 16, emphasis mine). It's my prayer that your students will come to the same conclusion as you dialogue about God's moral attributes.

BREAKING THE ICE
(10-12 MINUTES)

GLIMPSES OF GOD

Beforehand, write out the following attributes on index cards (one per card): HOLY, RIGHTEOUS, JUST, TRUTHFUL, and LOVING. Put the index cards in a box. When the session begins, have the students get into pairs and select a card from the box.

Say something like—

> **You all have a card with a characteristic of God written on it. Each of these characteristics shows us how God chooses to act or respond to us. I'd like you to come up with a short scene depicting how you think your attribute would play out in real life so we can get a glimpse of what God is like. Think of a situation you've experienced (or have**

witnessed someone else experience) and how
God responded with the attribute written on
your card. I'll give you about five minutes to
prepare, and then you'll act out your scene
for the rest of the group.

QUESTIONS TO ASK

1. Which attributes were the most difficult to act
   out? Why?
2. How do these moral actions look when they're
   used in human relationships, as compared with
   the way God acts them out?
3. What's the possibility of a human doing any of
   these things perfectly?

TRANSITIONAL TRUTH

Just by saying the word *perfectly*, we've admitted there's
a standard which we compare our lives. So we all have to
explain that standard in some way. If we go by the Bible,
then that standard is God—a tough act to follow! Let's keep
things in perspective. God is transcendent. That means God
is beyond our comprehension. We can't see or understand
God unless he exists and reveals himself to us. In the last
session, we learned some specific things about God's natural
attributes, but that list isn't comprehensive. We can't make
God into a product, put God in a box, or write out all God's
capabilities and components. But while God is transcendent
(completely beyond us and our comprehension), he's also
immanent (able to be with us).

   We take time to learn what we can about God, but
God should still be a mystery for each of us in some sense.
After all, he's God. A God whom Paul said is "over all and
through all and in all" (Ephesians 4:6). God wants us to
be full and complete, and we'll see how God completes us

through some of his moral characteristics—or the things that describe what God has determined to always be.

HEARING THE WORD
(8-10 MINUTES)

SEARCHING THE DEPTHS

Pass out copies of the **Searching the Depths** worksheet found on **page 85**. Have the students form groups of four or five to look up each passage and learn about a moral attribute of God. (Note: This activity will take longer than most. So depending on your time limitations, you may want to divide up the five sections and have each group take one or two.) When the students have finished their research, they'll describe the attribute in their own words. When the groups are done, bring them back together for a time of sharing.

Pass out copies of the **Searching the Depths** worksheet found on **page 85**.

TRANSITIONAL TRUTH

God has many characteristics, but it's important to remember that God is all of those things perfectly. We can see some of the same attributes in the world around us from time to time, but they're only a glimpse of the perfection found in God. God is perfectly holy, perfectly righteous, perfectly just, perfectly truthful, and perfectly loving. Let's take some more time to reflect upon the extent to which God loves us.

SHARING YOUR PERSPECTIVE
(9-10 MINUTES)

YOU'LL NEED

• A copy of the movie *Schindler's List* (Universal, 2003) and a way to show it

I COULD HAVE GOTTEN MORE!

Say something like—

> Throughout history certain people have done some amazing things that just blow our minds. One such person was Oskar Schindler. He risked his life to save hundreds of Jews who would have otherwise been victims of the Holocaust. We can get an idea of the extent of Schindler's compassion and desires from this video clip.

Play the clip from *Schindler's List* (scene 37; it ends when Schindler drives off). Please note that this movie is rated R. However, the Christian community embraced this film when it was released, and this specific clip has been chosen with a teenage audience in mind. You'll still want to view the clip in advance and use your own discretion in showing it to your students. You may even want to talk to another pastor or someone in authority at your church before using it.

QUESTIONS TO ASK

1. After all he'd done, what did Oskar Schindler realize when the people tried to honor him?
2. How has God shown his love and compassion for all human beings? For you?
3. Schindler said he could have done more. Do you think God can do more than he already has to show his love for you? If so, how?

TRANSITIONAL TRUTH

In a general sense, all of God's moral characteristics can be defined as "love." It really is all about love. First Corinthians 13 is a famous chapter in the Bible. It's sometimes referred to as the "love chapter." To see what love is like, let's compare Paul's description with our own lives. Whenever I see the word *love*, I'm going to insert my name to see how I measure up. You can do the same silently as I read.

(Read aloud 1 Corinthians 13:4-7 and insert your name.)

I don't know about you, but I don't come close. But there's Someone who does. In fact, he's perfect "love."

(Read 1 Corinthians 13:4-7 aloud again, but insert Jesus' name this time.)

God's love is perfect—as was shown through Jesus' life. In fact God takes it one step further—"Love [Jesus] never fails" (1 Corinthians 13:8). Only God could love so perfectly and without stopping. The question then is, *Where does that leave us?* We mentioned Tony Evans' statement (from *Our God Is Awesome*) in our first session, but it bears repeating: "Knowing who He is defines who we are." If this is true, then how does knowing that God is Love explain who we are?

MAKING IT PERSONAL
(7-10 MINUTES)

OPTION 1: I FOUND YOU JESUS

Say something like—

> **Take an index card and a pencil in hand while you listen to this song. Listen closely to the lyrics and write down at least one thought in the song that seems to relate to where you are. When the song is over, we'll share our thoughts with each other.**

Play the song "I Found You Jesus" by His Refuge and give students time to finish recording their thoughts after the song ends.

QUESTIONS TO ASK

1. **Which parts of the song did you connect with the most?**
2. **If you could write the lyrics of the song, what would you say?**
3. **If God loves you this much and this perfectly, then how should that change the way you live your life?**

OPTION 2: VISIONS OF LOVE

Have your students get back into their groups and look up 1 Corinthians 13:4-8. Using copies of the **Visions of Love** illustration handout, have them create a short comic or illustrated story based on the aspects of God's love that they see in the passage. They won't have time to get to them all so have them discuss and choose the ones that really impact them and create their illustration. When time is up, bring everyone together and have them share their illustrations.

BRINGING IT TOGETHER

If we understand all of what God is and what God is about, then we can know what God means to us. We can also know what we are and are not in light of God. God is everything we are not but *need* to be. We don't complete God—God is complete on his own. However, God certainly completes us. Notice how John says, "Love is made complete among us" (1 John 4:17). If we have a relationship with God, then we should be exhibiting this love in our lives.

Galatians 5:22-23 says that the fruit of the Holy Spirit is "love, joy, peace, patience, kindness, goodness, faithfulness, gentleness and self-control." Let's pray for friends and family who haven't experienced God's love. Let's also pray that we'll be an example of that great love to those around us.

SESSION 7: IT'S ALL ABOUT LOVE
SEARCHING THE DEPTHS
SMALL-GROUP WORKSHEET

Search the following Scripture passages to experience the depth of God's moral character. Write out your own personal definition of God's character for each section:

1. God is holy. Look up Isaiah 6:1-13 and 1 Peter 1:15-16 to get a picture of God's holiness.
   → Definition:

2. God is righteous. Look up Romans 3 and 2 Timothy 4:8 to learn what the Bible says about righteousness.
   → Definition:

3. God is just. Check out Deuteronomy 32:3-4 and Romans 3 to learn more concerning what it means to be just.
   → Definition:

4. God is truth. Look up references concerning the truth of God in Romans 3 and Titus 1:1-3.
   → Definition:

5. God is love. Complete your search by checking out Ephesians 2:1-7 and 1 John 4:7-21.
   → Definition:

SESSION 7: IT'S ALL ABOUT LOVE
SEARCHING THE DEPTHS
LEADER'S SMALL-GROUP WORKSHEET

Search the following Scripture passages to experience the depth of God's moral character. Write out your own personal definition of God's character for each section:

1. God is holy. Look up Isaiah 6:1-13 and 1 Peter 1:15-16 to get a picture of God's holiness.
   → Definition: *God is pure and set apart as something completely different or special.*

2. God is righteous. Look up Romans 3 and 2 Timothy 4:8 to learn what the Bible says about righteousness.
   → Definition: *God always does the right thing.*

3. God is just. Check out Deuteronomy 32:3-4 and Romans 3 to learn more concerning what it means to be just.
   → Definition: *God always judges according to the perfect standard.*

4. God is truth. Look up references concerning the truth of God in Romans 3 and Titus 1:1-3.
   → Definition: *God is the standard for what's right and wrong.*

5. God is love. Complete your search by checking out Ephesians 2:1-7 and 1 John 4:7-21.
   → Definition: *God actively seeks us out for relationship in spite of what we are or what we've done.*

SESSION 7: IT'S ALL ABOUT LOVE

VISIONS OF LOVE
ILLUSTRATION HANDOUT

According to 1 Corinthians 13:4-8, I believe that God is _____.
(Illustrate this in a comic sketch below.)

WHAT'S IN A NAME?

OVERVIEW

The focus of this lesson is a closer examination of the names used for God in Scripture. Students will learn some of the names of God, understand what they meant to people in Scripture, and apply the names of God to their personal prayer life.

SETTING THE TONE

Names are important. The meaning of a name seems to have lost some significance among parents who choose to name their child based upon contemporary culture. Yet there are still many parents who name a child in honor of a favorite relative or Bible character. Some go so far as to consider the importance and deeper meaning of family or biblical names when choosing a child's name. That's what my wife and I did. We chose our children's names after lots of discussion, and we landed on ones that were chock-full of meaning. It's an expression of their connection to our family. The names express our desire for each child to be in relationship with God and other people. In our minds, a name still says a lot about a child, even if you don't really know him or her yet.

It's not too different with God. Whether or not your students know God personally, they can get a good idea of who God is, where God came from, and what God will do by considering not only the names he's given himself, but also the names God's people have applied to him throughout history. Encourage your students to refer to God by one of his many names. In doing so, they may find that all they need can be found in God's name.

BREAKING THE ICE
(7-10 MINUTES)

OPTION 1: WHAT'S MY NAME?

Have your students grab some paper and pencils and number their sheets from one to 10. As you read the statements from the **What's My Name?** game sheet on **page 96,** have students write down their answers. Go over the answers at the end and reward your group's pop icon guru.

QUESTIONS TO ASK

1. **Why do you think these people chose to use another name?**
2. **What's the significance of the names they chose?**
3. **What can you learn about people from their names?**

OPTION 2: MY NAME IS INIGO MONTOYA

Introduce the clip from *The Princess Bride* by saying something like—

> **After our hero Westley (played by Cary Elwes) has finally made it to the top of the Cliffs of Insanity, he's graciously given a moment to rest and get to know his opponent—an expert swordsman who intends to fight him to the death. During this brief conversation, his adversary reveals something very important to him.**

YOU'LL NEED

• A copy of the movie *The Princess Bride* (MGM, 1987) and a way to show it

Play the clip (from 0:19:26 to 0:21:21). There's another great scene at the end of the movie when Inigo (played by Mandy Patinkin) faces off with Count Rugen (played by Christopher Guest), the six-fingered man. Watch both clips ahead of time and decide if you like that one better or wish to show both.

QUESTIONS TO ASK

1. **Why is Inigo's name so important to his revenge against the six-fingered man?**
2. **What does a name represent?**
3. **How can you get to know someone by her name or even by the nickname she uses instead?**

TRANSITIONAL TRUTH

Proverbs 22:1 says, "A good name is more desirable than great riches; to be esteemed is better than silver or gold." While this Scripture applies more to the testimony or reputation of an individual, a name can also reflect on the parents' hopes for the child. Sometimes it just gives us an idea of where the person grew up or what kind of lifestyle someone had. Let's think through a few examples.

SHARING YOUR PERSPECTIVE
(8-10 MINUTES)

GOOD, BAD, AND UGLY NAMES

In advance prepare a way to display the Biblical and group names and their meanings. Whether it's PowerPoint slides, overhead pages, or a simple poster, this visual aspect will help many of your students make a connection with the importance of names.

Begin the discussion of names by talking about the meanings of a few biblical names:

> **Throughout the Bible we read about the importance of a person's name. Here are a few examples of biblical names, their meanings, and how they reflected or impacted the life story of the person:**
>
> - **A man in the Old Testament named Laban had two famous daughters, both of whom Jacob married. (Yes, there are some strange stories in the Bible.) Rachel means "a little lamb." Leah means "cow or weary one." Which one did Jacob actually want to marry?** *(Rachel, but he was tricked by their father into marrying Leah, the older sister, first.)*
> - **There were two men who spent some time in prison together because of their witness for Jesus Christ. The name Paul means "little one." The name Silas means "wood."**
> - **Jesus gave one of his disciples, Simon, a new name. When Simon came to follow Jesus, he was given the name Peter, which means "rock" (John 1:42). Later, when Peter declared that Jesus is the Messiah, Jesus said Peter was the rock on which he would build his church (Matthew 16:18).**

Help this illustration really hit home by doing some research on the meanings of the names of the students in your group and sharing the results with everyone. (Note: You may want to check with your students before you share the meaning of their names—just to be sure no one is sensitive about their name or embarrassed by the meaning.) There are all kinds of baby-name Web sites that will provide you with the meanings of names. You may also want to ask a couple of students if they have a special story about the meaning of their name and would be willing to share it with the group.

QUESTIONS TO ASK

1. **Why do you think someone would choose a certain name?**
2. **Why you were given your name?**
3. **Tell about someone you know whose life reflected or contrasted with his or her name.**
4. **How can knowing God's names help us understand who God is?**

TRANSITIONAL TRUTH

If our names can mean so much, then it seems only natural that God's name would tell us a lot about him. The interesting thing about the name of God is that he doesn't have just one. "Yahweh" is the most consistent name used, but God has been given many names over the course of history. We'll take a look at a few of them, but keep this in mind as you read: Unlike some people's names, God's names actually *do* tell us who God *is*, and God is all the things those names describe, *perfectly*.

HEARING THE WORD
(8-10 MINUTES)

ONE GOD, MANY NAMES

Pass out copies of the **One God, Many Names** worksheet found on **page 97**. Have the students form groups of four or five to look up each passage, learn more about some of the names of God, and describe the attributes in their own words. When the groups are finished, bring them back together for a time of sharing.

YOU'LL NEED

• Copies of the **One God, Many Names** worksheet, one for each smaller group of students

• Pencils

• Bibles

• A copy of the "Names of God" video from Highway Video (*Vibe Video Vol. 4*) and a way to show it

TRANSITIONAL TRUTH

Say something like—

Let's take time to just reflect upon some of the names of God. Sit silently and watch this clip.

Show the "Names of God" video. Or you may choose to make your own multimedia presentation with the names of God used in this lesson set to music.

MAKING IT PERSONAL
(15-20 MINUTES)

IN HIS NAME D

This prayer activity will serve as both the "Making It Personal" and "Bringing It Together" sections for this lesson. Let's allow the Holy Spirit to lead our students in bringing this one together through their prayers.

Pass out copies of the **In His Name** prayer sheet found on **page 99** and ask students to break into groups of two or three. Say—

> Take some time to read over these names of God with your group. Once you've read through them, spend the rest of your time together praying through the names of God, offering thanks for who God is and asking for God's personal touch on your lives in a specific way. When you've finished, you're welcome to leave or wait silently while others are praying.

YOU'LL NEED

- Copies of the **In His Name** prayer sheet, one for each smaller group of students

SESSION 8: WHAT'S IN A NAME?

WHAT'S MY NAME?
GAME SHEET

Read the following statements aloud and have the students write down their guess for which famous person is being described. When you've finished, go through them again and provide the answers. Reward the student who came up with the most correct answers.

- My real name is Paul Hewson. I'm a major political spokesperson, even though my main career is as a lead vocalist for a well-known band. *(Answer: Bono)*

- My real last name is Lipschitz, but my clothing line wouldn't be very popular with that name written on it, do you think? *(Answer: Ralph Lauren)*

- You're definitely more familiar with my stage name than my real name: Carlos Irwin Estévez. I'm one of Two and a Half funny men. *(Answer: Charlie Sheen)*

- Florian Cloud de Bounevialle O'Malley Armstrong—quite a mouthful! I shortened it before I sang about my "Life for Rent". *(Answer: Dido)*

- Marshall Bruce Mathers III sounded too regal for my line of work. Oh, and my name's not really Slim Shady, either. *(Answer: Eminem)*

- I was born with four names. I kept my first and last names, but I had to simplify by getting rid of the two names in between: Columcille and Gerard. I just wasn't passionate about such a long, awkward name. *(Answer: Mel Gibson)*

- Here I am now going to the South Side and known by my family as Richard Melville Hall. *(Answer: Moby)*

- My musical stage name doesn't show it, but I'm proud of my Latino background. Enrique Morales just wasn't catchy. *(Answer: Ricky Martin)*

- Alecia Moore is my real name, but I'm still no Britney Spears. Let's get this party started! *(Answer: Pink)*

SESSION 8: WHAT'S IN A NAME?

ONE GOD, MANY NAMES
SMALL-GROUP WORKSHEET

Take a look at some of the names for God. Look up each passage and write out what you think each name tells us about the character of God.

1. Yahweh (OT): Exodus 3:14-15 (NLT)
   God is…
   (Note: *Jehovah* is a misreading of the Hebrew text for *Yahweh*, but it's commonly used as a name of God. In your English Bibles, *Yahweh* is what's translated as LORD.)

2. El Shaddai (OT): Genesis 17:1 (NLT)
   God is…

3. Adonai (OT) or Kurios (NT): Isaiah 6:8 and Matthew 23:10
   God is…

4. Elohim (OT) or Theos (NT): Genesis 1:1 and John 20:28
   God is…

5. El Elyon (OT): Isaiah 14:13-14
   God is…

6. El Roi (OT): Genesis 16:13-14
   God is…

7. Immanuel (OT and NT): Isaiah 7:14 and Matthew 1:23
   God is…

8. Pater (NT): Luke 11:2 and John 1:12
   God is…

SESSION 8: WHAT'S IN A NAME?
ONE GOD, MANY NAMES
LEADER'S SMALL-GROUP WORKSHEET

Take a look at some of the names for God. Look up each passage and write out what you think each name tells us about the character of God.

1. Yahweh (OT): Exodus 3:14-15 (NLT)
   God is...*I AM, or always existing in the present state.*
   (Note: *Jehovah* is a misreading of the Hebrew text for *Yahweh*, but it's commonly used as a name of God. In your English Bibles, *Yahweh* is what's translated as LORD.)

2. El Shaddai (OT): Genesis 17:1 (NLT)
   God is...*Almighty, or able to do anything.*

3. Adonai (OT) or Kurios (NT): Isaiah 6:8 and Matthew 23:10
   God is...*Lord, or the One who has authority over my life.*

4. Elohim (OT) or Theos (NT): Genesis 1:1 and John 20:28
   God is...*God, or One who is greater than we are.*

5. El Elyon (OT): Isaiah 14:13-14
   God is...*Most High, or above all things.*

6. El Roi (OT): Genesis 16:13-14
   God is...*the One who sees me.*

7. Immanuel (OT and NT): Isaiah 7:14 and Matthew 1:23
   God is...*with us.*

8. Pater (NT): Luke 11:2 and John 1:12
   God is...*our Father.*

SESSION 8: WHAT'S IN A NAME?
IN HIS NAME
PRAYER SHEET

With a partner, pray over some of the names of God. Below are some verses that talk about each name. Take your time with this. Think about what each name means for you, truly thank God, and be encouraged because of who God is.

- God is our Provider (Yahweh-Jireh)
  Genesis 22:14—"So Abraham called that place The LORD Will Provide. And to this day it is said, 'On the mountain of the LORD it will be provided.'"

- God is our Healer (Yahweh-Rophe)
  Exodus 15:26—"He said, 'If you listen carefully to the LORD your God and do what is right in his eyes, if you pay attention to his commands and keep all his decrees, I will not bring on you any of the diseases I brought on the Egyptians, for I am the LORD, who heals you.'"

- God is our Peace (Yahweh-Shalom)
  Judges 6:22-24—"When Gideon realized that it was the angel of the LORD, he exclaimed, 'Ah, Sovereign LORD! I have seen the angel of the LORD face to face!' But the LORD said to him, 'Peace! Do not be afraid. You are not going to die.' So Gideon built an altar to the LORD there and called it The LORD Is Peace. To this day it stands in Ophrah of the Abiezrites."

- God is our Shepherd (Yahweh-Rohi)
  Psalm 23:1—"The LORD is my shepherd, I lack nothing."

- God is our Righteousness (Yahweh-Tsidkenu)
  Jeremiah 23:6—"In his days Judah will be saved and Israel will live in safety. This is the name by which he will be called: The LORD Our Righteous Savior."

WHO'S IN CONTROL?

OVERVIEW

The focus of this lesson is on the sovereignty of God. Students will learn to define God's sovereignty, understand their need for God's direction, and determine to live in recognition of God's sovereignty.

SETTING THE TONE

"You are in control of your own destiny." That's what students hear, but that's not what the Bible teaches. Throughout Scripture God continually reminds his people who is in control. Take the story of Gideon, for example. God told him he had too many men, even though Gideon's enemies already outnumbered him. Some say God wanted only the best men. I believe God had Gideon make the cuts so everyone involved would know that victory was only possible because of God.

Jesus encourages us to submit to God and "lose our lives." Each of us needs to come to a place where we realize our life is not our own. God is in control. We can fool ourselves for a while, but one day everyone will know full well the sovereignty of God. And yet, it's nothing to fear or fight against. We should embrace God's rule in our lives, knowing God will do what's best. It's not easy, but we need to keep reminding ourselves—and our students—that, in spite of what people say, God is sovereign. *God* is the one in control of our destinies.

BREAKING THE ICE
(8-10 MINUTES)

LEADING THE PACK

Make copies of the **Leading the Pack** sheet on **page 108** and cut each one into strips so you have one strip for each student. Have the students break into groups of three or four. Tell them they're to follow the directions on their slips of paper but keep their own job descriptions to themselves. (*Yes, the descriptions are all the same, but the students won't know that.*) Let them go for about five minutes to see how the students deal with the issues that come up.

QUESTIONS TO ASK

1. **How do you feel this activity went?**
2. **What do you think made it easy or difficult?** (*If they haven't figured it out yet, let them know at this point that they all had the same job description.*)
3. **What could you do differently if you had it to do all over again?**
4. **How does what we've talked about here relate to our study of God?**
5. **When it comes to the plans you make in your life,**

do you usually consider yourself or God to be the one in control?

TRANSITIONAL TRUTH

Let's say you receive $10,000. Would you be willing to let me tell you what to do with the money? Not likely. You'd want to make the decision about how to spend what's yours—it's only natural. But this concept can help us gain a better understanding of God's sovereignty, or control, in our lives.

Romans 9:20-21 states, "But who are you, a mere human being, to talk back to God? 'Shall what is formed say to the one who formed it, "Why did you make me like this?"' Does not the potter have the right to make out of the same lump of clay some pottery for noble purposes and some for disposal of refuse?" God has a right to do whatever he wants with what's his. And we are his.

SHARING YOUR PERSPECTIVE
(10-12 MINUTES)

PLAYING IT OUT

YOU'LL NEED

• A Bible, or Matthew 20:1-16 printed on a sheet of paper

Tell your students you want them to act out a story from the Bible to help them understand how God's sovereignty can look in our lives and in the lives of those around us. Choose students to play the following parts: Landowner, workers, idle people, and supervisor. Give the landowner a handful of dollar bills as props. Then read aloud Matthew 20:1-16 and have your students act out the story, repeating any of the dialogue after you.

QUESTIONS TO ASK

1. The workers: **Is the payment fair in your minds?**
2. All students: **Was the payment just (right according to the standard)?**
3. The landowner: **How does this relate to what God chooses to do?**
4. All students: **How difficult is it to accept this aspect of God?**
5. All students: **What are some benefits?**

TRANSITIONAL TRUTH

Some of you may have seen the bumper sticker that says GOD IS MY COPILOT. What do you think that statement means to the person driving the car? Considering God's sovereignty, what's the problem with that statement? Basically, if God is your copilot, then you'd better change seats. Life is much different if we submit to God's authority rather than our own. Let's see what Scripture has to say about God's sovereignty.

YOU'LL NEED

- Copies of the **God Is My PILOT** worksheet, one for each student
- Pencils
- Bibles

HEARING THE WORD
(8-10 MINUTES)

GOD IS MY PILOT

Have the students get into small groups and hand each student a copy of the **God Is My PILOT** worksheet on **page 109**. Give them time to answer the questions. And when most of the groups have finished, have each group share a couple of their answers with everyone.

TRANSITIONAL TRUTH

We often believe we're entitled to whatever we want. And this is true whether or not we're children of God. It can be hard to give up control of our lives, but it can also be very freeing. As children of God, we have access to the benefits of God's gifts and desires for us—things we'd never come up with on our own.

In his book *It's Not About Me*, Max Lucado asks, "Do you really want the world to revolve around you? If it's all about you, then it's all up to you. Your Father rescues you from such a burden." You see, the great part is that God chooses. God purposefully chose to make you the way you are, and God wants to use you in wonderful ways—if you'll allow him. Philippians 1:6 says we can be "confident of this, that he who began a good work in you will carry it on to completion until the day of Christ Jesus."

MAKING IT PERSONAL
(7-8 MINUTES)

OPTION 1: THE CLAY

Play the video "The Clay."

QUESTIONS TO ASK

1 **What do you think about the idea of "yielding" yourself to God?**

2. How do you think you can be too soft for God to mold you?
3. What does the person look like who is "usable" clay?

Say something like—

> Don't answer out loud, but what kind of clay do you think you are right now? Take the next two to three minutes to talk to God about where you are in your life. I'll finish with a prayer for everyone.

YOU'LL NEED

• Three lumps of clay, prepared in advance

OPTION 2: MOLDABLE

Before leading today's session, purchase some clay and separate it into three chunks. Leave one out to dry for a few days. Put one into a bucket of water until it's very soft. Leave the other one alone until just before this session, then spend a few minutes working it in your hands to soften it. Set out the three lumps of clay for students to feel or pass them around your group. Allow them to touch, hold, and squeeze each lump of clay.

QUESTIONS TO ASK

1. Which lump of clay would be the easiest to mold into something you wanted to create?
2. What would be the challenges of working with the other two lumps?
3. The Bible refers to God as the "potter" and us as "clay." What does it look like to be usable clay to God? What can make us too hard or too soft?

Say something like—

> Don't answer out loud, but what kind of clay do you think you are right now? Take

the next two to three minutes to talk to God about where you are in your life. I'll finish with a prayer for everyone.

BRINGING IT TOGETHER

God is in control. God has the right to do whatever he wants with what's his—and everything is God's. God may allow us to try to control our lives; but because we're human and sinful, we'll always mess things up. The good news is we don't have to keep fighting for control—we can give it to the One who really has it in the first place. Living in the truth of God's sovereignty can be scary at times, but it's also very freeing. If we submit to God's authority, the Holy Spirit will "guide [us] into all the truth" (John 16:13). And remember, nothing is impossible…with God. Keep that in mind over the coming week.

SESSION 9: WHO'S IN CONTROL?

LEADING THE PACK
BREAKING THE ICE ACTIVITY

Your team is responsible for planning an awesome weekend retreat for our group. You're the **LEADER** of this project. Others may want to lead, but you need to be sure to keep control of your group if you're to be successful. Be sure everyone in your group has a job and you're able to explain your plan clearly when I call on your group.

Your team is responsible for planning an awesome weekend retreat for our group. You're the **LEADER** of this project. Others may want to lead, but you need to be sure to keep control of your group if you're to be successful. Be sure everyone in your group has a job and you're able to explain your plan clearly when I call on your group.

Your team is responsible for planning an awesome weekend retreat for our group. You're the **LEADER** of this project. Others may want to lead, but you need to be sure to keep control of your group if you're to be successful. Be sure everyone in your group has a job and you're able to explain your plan clearly when I call on your group.

Your team is responsible for planning an awesome weekend retreat for our group. You're the **LEADER** of this project. Others may want to lead, but you need to be sure to keep control of your group if you're to be successful. Be sure everyone in your group has a job and you're able to explain your plan clearly when I call on your group.

SESSION 9: WHO'S IN CONTROL?
GOD IS MY PILOT
SMALL-GROUP WORKSHEET

In your small group, work through the questions below. As you consider each question, write a personal application—for YOUR life. Be prepared to share some thoughts when everyone is finished.

1. What is God's? (Psalm 24:1)

2. (Circle one) T or F—You are your own person. Explain your answer below. (1 Corinthians 6:19-20)

3. What does God want to happen with what belongs to him? (Ephesians 1:9-12)

4. The word for *will* is used four times in Ephesians 1, and *pleasure* is mentioned twice. Both hold the same concept of God's decision or will. What are the benefits we receive as a result of God's control?

5. In what areas of your life can you see God's control? What might be some areas you still need to surrender to God? (The more you're willing to share with your group, the more opportunity you'll have for prayer support and perhaps wisdom from someone who's already been through it.)

SESSION 9: WHO'S IN CONTROL?

GOD IS MY PILOT
LEADER'S SMALL-GROUP WORKSHEET

In your small group, work through the questions below. As you consider each question, write a personal application—for YOUR life. Be prepared to share some thoughts when everyone is finished.

1. What is God's? (Psalm 24:1)
   The earth and everything in it! (Does that leave out the rest of the universe?)

2. (Circle one) T or F—You are your own person. Explain your answer below.
   1 Corinthians 6:19-20)
   TRUE if we listen to those around us.
   FALSE according to the Scriptures, as we belong to God.

3. What does God want to happen with what belongs to him? (Ephesians 1:9-12)
   Some possible responses:
   (1) God wants us all to be together under Jesus,
   (2) God wants us all to praise him.

4. The word for *will* is used four times in Ephesians 1, and *pleasure* is mentioned twice. Both hold the same concept of God's decision or will. What are the benefits we receive as a result of God's control?
   Possible responses: Adoption, redemption, grace, being sealed as God's

5. In what areas of your life can you see God's control? What might be some areas you still need to surrender to God? (The more you're willing to share with your group, the more opportunity you'll have for prayer support and perhaps wisdom from someone who's already been through it.)
   The more open you are, the more your students will be willing to open up.

GOD'S MYSTERIOUS WILL

OVERVIEW

This lesson provides a brief look at the will of God. Students will learn ways to determine God's will, understand how to live within God's will, and commit to following God's will with their life decisions.

SETTING THE TONE

"How can I know God's will for my life?" How many times have you heard this question? Everyone is looking for a personalized plan from God that's sent to them in some divine fashion so they can follow it to the letter. I don't think that's what God has in mind. In his book *The Mystery of God's Will*, Charles Swindoll says, "God's will for us in this life is not some black-and-white objective equation designed to take us to an appointed destination here on earth as much as it is about the journey itself."

So let's focus on hearing God as we travel. God has already revealed his general will for us in his Word. If we follow God's Word, we'll be "in God's will." Jesus did this. When the Jews questioned how Jesus could know so much without taking as much time to study God's Word as they had,

> Jesus answered, "My teaching is not my own. It comes from the one who sent me. Anyone who chooses to do the will of God will find out whether my teaching comes from God or whether I speak on my own. Whoever speaks on their own does so to gain personal glory, but he who seeks the glory of the one who sent him is a man of truth; there is nothing false about him. Has not Moses given you the law? Yet not one of you keeps the law." (John 7:16-19)

Jesus basically said that his words would be true to a people who were in God's will. These people had God's will, but they weren't following it. The same is true today. It seems to take the mystery out of it, right? Unless…the mystery is in how God moves you while your eyes are focused on what God's already revealed to be his will. Hmmm?

Like I've said before, it's not about us. It's all about God. Let's lead our students to focus on God and his will, as opposed to their personalized, specialized, all-about-my-life will.

BREAKING THE ICE
(7-8 MINUTES)

IF YOU BUILD IT...

Begin by showing a clip from *Evan Almighty* (0:30:10 to 0:33:37). The clip ends when God has vanished and Evan thinks, *That is just cruel.*

QUESTIONS TO ASK

1. Evan asks, "Why are you doing this?" What do you think he's feeling at that point?
2. Why do you think God does what he does?
3. God laughs when Evan talks about "his" plans. Why do you think God did this?
4. Did God clearly lay out a plan for how to accomplish change? What was it?
5. How is this interaction between God and Evan like or unlike our personal interactions with the true God?

YOU'LL NEED

• A copy of the movie *Evan Almighty* (Universal, 2007) and a way to show it

TRANSITIONAL TRUTH

The will of God is mysterious in some ways, and people are always trying to figure it out. A will can be explained as something one wishes to do or has determined will be. If we could know what God wants to do with us, then we could better understand how to jump on board with his plan. What if God has already told us his will? What if it's bigger than us and we've just missed it because we're looking for something with our name on it?

YOU'LL NEED

- Copies of the **God's Will—Defined** worksheet, one for each smaller group of students
- Pencils
- Bibles

HEARING THE WORD
(8-10 MINUTES)

DEFINING A WILL

Have the students get into pairs or small groups. Hand each group a copy of the **God's Will—Defined** worksheet on **page 119** and give them time to answer the questions. When most of the groups have finished, have each group share their answers to a couple of the questions with everyone.

TRANSITIONAL TRUTH

We can find God's will written out for us in his Word. God's will for our lives isn't a mystery, though his *ways* may very well be. God's desire for our lives is more of an open book that needs to be read and applied. Paul said in the closing verses of his letter to the Romans, "Now to him who is able to establish you by my gospel and the proclamation of Jesus Christ, according to the revelation of the mystery hidden for long ages past, but *now revealed and made known through the prophetic writings by the command of the eternal God*, so that all nations might believe and obey him—to the only wise God be glory forever through Jesus Christ! Amen." Now the question isn't so much, "What is God's will for my life?" but, "How can I live according to God's will?"

SHARING YOUR PERSPECTIVE
(15-20 MINUTES)

WILLFUL ACTIONS

Have the students pair up with a new partner and prepare to role-play how they'd make a decision based upon the guidelines discussed earlier for understanding and following God's will. You can give them a couple of ideas for the scenario (being encouraged by a friend to have sex, choosing a college, deciding whether to attend a party), but it's best if they come up with the scenario themselves. This will provide greater insight for you to know what kinds of things they're dealing with. Give the students five to six minutes to come up with a plan, and then provide time for each pair to present their role-play for everyone. (If you have a larger group, divide your students into small groups instead of pairs.)

QUESTIONS TO ASK

1. **How real are these situations in your personal lives?**
2. **What went through your mind as you thought about how a situation like this might play out in real life?**
3. **Don't answer this question out loud: Where do you think you are right now in your commitment to following the will of God?**

TRANSITIONAL TRUTH

Paul seems to relay God's desire for all his people in Colossians 4:12: "Epaphras, who is one of you and a

servant of Christ Jesus, sends greetings. He is always wrestling in prayer for you, that you may stand firm in all the will of God, mature and fully assured."

God wants to complete the Word in you, and I share God's heart in seeing you become strong and fully assured. The best way to start is to think through what this means to you personally and how committed you want to be in following God's will.

MAKING IT PERSONAL
(7-10 MINUTES)

OPTION 1: WHERE AM I WITH GOD? 🄳 ✋

Invite your students to spread out around the room. Ask them to remain standing for now. When all your students have found a place, say—

> Think about what it means not just to follow God's will but to really *be* in God's will. Romans 12:1-2 says, "Therefore, I urge you, brothers and sisters, in view of God's mercy, to offer your bodies as a living sacrifice, holy and pleasing to God—this is true worship. Do not conform to the pattern of this world, but be transformed by the renewing of your mind. Then you will be able to test and approve what God's will is—his good, pleasing and perfect will."

> God's will is not something he is hiding from you. He wants you to know and live in it. However, we aren't always in a place to see or understand it. Let's take some

time to pray. As we pray, I'm going to ask you to take a prayer posture that represents where you feel you are with God. First, close your eyes. Now, listen as I read some questions and descriptions to get you thinking about your relationship to God. When you feel like what I'm describing fits you, follow the instructions for that particular posture. When everyone is in place, we'll spend a few minutes in silent prayer, and then I'll close for us as a group."

QUESTIONS TO ASK

1. Have you been conforming more to the pressures of sin and ungodliness? Perhaps you need to come to God today in humility and offer yourself as a "living sacrifice." If this is where you are, lay down on the floor.

2. Are you desiring to live for God but finding yourself stuck or feeling like the Christian life is stale and boring? Perhaps you need to experience that transforming power of God and a renewal of your mind and spirit. If this is where you are, sit down.

3. Are you in a place where you are hearing and moving in and living in the will of God with some level of confidence? Perhaps you need to take time to offer praise to God for what He has done in your life. Remain standing, but place your hands in the air in a posture of praise to your God.

4. Maybe you don't know where you fit into this mix. That's okay. If you haven't taken another posture, you can get down on your knees and ask that God show you where you are and how you should respond to his will.

After the students have had a few minutes of silent prayer, conclude this time with a personal prayer for your group, and bring them back together to wrap things up.

OPTION 2: UNCONTROLLABLE CURRENT

Show the video "Uncontrollable Current."

QUESTIONS TO ASK

1. How do you relate to the man in this clip?
2. What do you think will happen as you submit to God's will?
3. Where will this man end up? What about you?
4. Why can you be at peace when making such a decision? Or can you?

BRINGING IT TOGETHER

We've come a long way on our journey to understand more about God—from talking about how we can know God exists to surrendering our lives completely to God's will. So how can all this change our daily lives? Yes, we'll still have to make choices. Submitting to God's will doesn't mean sitting back and doing nothing. But as we align our choices with the guidelines God has given us in the Bible and submit to God's desires for us, we can live in freedom and experience his peace. As we get ready to go, let me read Colossians 4:12 again. But this time I'm going to personalize it. I want you to know that you're not alone on your journey. "(Your name), who is one of you and a servant of Christ Jesus, sends greetings. I am always wrestling in prayer for you, that you may stand firm in all the will of God, mature and fully assured." Let me end with just such a prayer for you right now.

SESSION 10:
GOD'S MYSTERIOUS WILL

GOD'S WILL—DEFINED
SMALL-GROUP WORKSHEET

The following verses contain references to the will of God. Look up each verse and write in the space provided how you think it defines God's will.

1. John 6:40; Galatians 1:4-5

2. Hebrews 10:36; 1 John 2:17

3. Ephesians 1:1; Colossians 1:1; 2 Timothy 1:1

4. Romans 1:10; 1 Peter 3:17

5. Ephesians 6:5-8; Matthew 16:27

SESSION 10:
GOD'S MYSTERIOUS WILL
GOD'S WILL—DEFINED
LEADER'S SMALL-GROUP WORKSHEET

The following verses contain references to the will of God. Look up each verse and write in the space provided how you think it defines God's will.

1. John 6:40; Galatians 1:4-5
   Possible response: God's will is for us to receive life or to be rescued from death.

2. Hebrews 10:36; 1 John 2:17
   Possible response: God's will is for us to follow him to the end.

3. Ephesians 1:1; Colossians 1:1; 2 Timothy 1:1
   Possible response: God's will determines what we do or how we'll serve him.

4. Romans 1:10; 1 Peter 3:17
   Possible response: God's will determines whether we'll suffer hardship.

5. Ephesians 6:5-8; Matthew 16:27
   Possible response: It is God's will that we do good, acting from a pure heart. God will determine how we are rewarded for serving him and doing what God says in his Word.

OVERVIEW

This lesson provides a reflective look at our place in God's kingdom. Students will learn how the kingdom begins, reflect on their place in God's kingdom, and visualize what they want to do with their lives as a result of God's invitation to enter his kingdom.

SETTING THE TONE

Once we have a good understanding of the fact that God is in control, we can focus on God's desire for those who submit to his authority. But in order to understand life within God's kingdom, we need to look at some practical ways in which that plays out in real life.

In his book *The Kingdom Agenda: What a Way to Live!* Tony Evans explains:

> Throughout the Bible, the kingdom of God is his rule, his plan, his program. God's kingdom is all-embracing. It covers everything in the universe. In fact, we can define God's kingdom as his comprehensive rule over all creation. It is the rule of God (theocracy) and not the rule of man (homocracy) that is paramount. Now if God's kingdom is comprehensive, so is his kingdom agenda. The kingdom agenda, then, may be defined as *the visible demonstration of the comprehensive rule of God over every area of life.*

Since we've already talked about what God controls and God's will, we're focusing here on the "visible demonstration" of that reality. This can be a tricky topic because we're really spending time looking at the "outside" of our lives and the lives of others. When Jesus spoke of these things, he didn't refer to a list of bullet points to follow—he provided illustrations. The goal with this lesson is the same. The way people's lives look on the outside is going to vary, even if they're in a group of people who all submit to God's authority. Such is the beauty of God's design! So encourage your students to begin thinking about how they personally fit into the kingdom.

BREAKING THE ICE
(7-8 MINUTES)

ROYALTY FOR A DAY

Ask your students—If you were king or queen for a day, what would you do? Allow plenty of time for thoughts and responses. If the students are having a hard time, you can ask some follow-up questions:

- **What law might you create or change?**
- **Who would you like to recognize or help?** *(This could be an individual or a group of people.)*
- **How would you live your life in that one day?**

TRANSITIONAL TRUTH

Merriam-Webster defines *kingdom* as "a politically organized community or major territorial unit having a monarchical form of government headed by a king or queen." God's kingdom could be called "a spiritually organized community having a monarchical form of government headed by a King." That's right, it's not a democracy. We don't have a vote. The orders come from above—from our King. There are some different references to the kingdom of God in Scripture, and we'd do well to think through what those references mean and how we might find our place in God's kingdom.

SHARING YOUR PERSPECTIVE
(8-10 MINUTES)

WHICH KINGDOM IS WHICH?

(Note: You'll want to prepare ahead of time by going through this sheet on your own.) People have varying views of when certain aspects of God's kingdom exist, so be sure to consider where you and your church stand on some of these areas. The point with this small-group activity is to expose students to the different uses of the term *kingdom* and encourage them to begin forming their beliefs about the kingdom.

Have the students get into small groups and hand each group a copy of the **Which Kingdom Is Which?** worksheet on **page 129**. Give them time to answer the questions. When most of the groups have finished, have each group share a couple of their answers with everyone.

TRANSITIONAL TRUTH

In spite of the different references to a kingdom, there seems to be a common general process that occurs when someone becomes a part of it. Now, not everyone will go through the process in the same way. But Jesus does give us a basic principle of response to his invitation for us to become a part of his eternal kingdom. As we look at these concepts, we need to consider where we are in relation to God's eternal kingdom.

HEARING THE WORD
(12-15 MINUTES)

A VISUAL TOUR OF THE KINGDOM'S BEGINNING—PART 1

Take some time to talk through Matthew 13:1-9 with your students. Below is a list of the main points of the story. Before your time together, find images on the Internet that correspond with each of the points of the story. Either print the pictures or project them for students to see as you read and talk through Matthew 13:1-9. The point of the pictures is to help solidify the story in their minds and to help them remember the lessons they learned the next time they see a similar

YOU'LL NEED
- Pictures from the Internet
- Bibles

image. Connecting the message of the kingdom with things your students are regularly exposed to in their everyday lives provides an opportunity to reinforce their learning outside of your time together. It's how Jesus taught! As you go, be sure to allow students to interact with the pictures and statements.

MAIN POINTS FROM MATTHEW 13

- A farmer went out to sow his seed. (v. 3)
- Some fell along the path, and the birds came and ate it up. (v. 4) [v. 19]
- Some fell on rocky places; it sprang up quickly and when the sun came, the plants were scorched and they withered. (vv. 5-6) [vv. 20-21]
- Other seed fell among thorns, which grew up and choked the plants. (v. 7) [v. 22]
- Still other seed fell on good soil, where it produced a crop—100, 60, or 30 times what was sown. (v. 8) [v. 23]
- He who has ears, let him hear. (v. 9)

QUESTIONS TO ASK

1. **How many of you have ears?**
2. **How many of you heard and understood that?**

A VISUAL TOUR OF THE KINGDOM'S BEGINNING—PART 2

Take your students through the pictures again. This time, have a student read the corresponding verses found in brackets (above), which give Jesus' explanation of each of the points of the parable.

QUESTIONS TO ASK

1. What's the one thing that's consistent in each of the situations?
2. What are the variables or differences?
3. What do you think the ground or soil refers to?
4. Don't answer out loud, but which one of the scenarios do you think best explains where you are today?

TRANSITIONAL TRUTH

God has invited everyone to be a part of his kingdom. The best expression of his desire was through his Son, Jesus Christ. In John 3:16-21, Jesus explains God's passion to Nicodemus:

> For God so loved the world that he gave his one and only Son, that whoever believes in him shall not perish but have eternal life. For God did not send his Son into the world to condemn the world, but to save the world through him. Whoever believes in him is not condemned, but whoever does not believe stands condemned already because they have not believed in the name of God's one and only Son. This is the verdict: Light has come into the world, but people loved darkness instead of light because their deeds were evil. All those who do evil hate the light, and will not come into the light for fear that their deeds will be exposed. But those who live by the truth come into the light, so that it may be seen plainly that what they have done has been done in the sight of God.

You see, God wants everyone to experience his love and care. Yet how can people expect to be cared for by the King if they're not living in his kingdom? Let's take a few minutes to reflect upon where each of us is in relation to God's kingdom.

MAKING IT PERSONAL
(9-10 MINUTES)

MY PLACE IN THE KINGDOM D ✋

YOU'LL NEED
- Construction paper
- Markers

Pass out construction paper and markers for the students to use as they create some drawings. Say something like—

> We've looked at a lot of pictures to show how God's kingdom begins. As you consider your place in God's kingdom, you'll be creating your own picture. Don't put your name on it. Just draw a line down the middle of the page. On the left side, draw an illustration of how you see yourself—in or out of God's kingdom. On the right side, draw a picture of where you'd like to be. How would you like to be living in relation to God's kingdom? When you've finished, pass your picture over to me. When everyone is done, we'll look at the pictures and use them to guide our prayers.

After the students have completed their pictures, display them one at a time for the rest of the class. You might ask some students to share what they see in the picture, and then ask for someone to pray for the person that picture represents.

BRINGING IT TOGETHER

We'll close by repeating the words of Jesus as he instructed his disciples to pray in Matthew 6:9-13. Read with me in your Bibles and let this be your prayer as you leave: "Our Father in heaven, hallowed be your name, your kingdom come, your will be done, on earth as it is in heaven. Give us today our daily bread. And forgive us our debts, as we also have forgiven our debtors. And lead us not into temptation, but deliver us from the evil one." Amen.

SESSION 11: KINGDOM LIFE
WHICH KINGDOM IS WHICH?
SMALL-GROUP WORKSHEET

1. What are some of the major components of a kingdom?

2. What is God's kingdom according to 1 Chronicles 29:11? How long does it last (Psalm 145:13)?

3. What's the kingdom like that God has promised to set up here on earth (2 Samuel 7:12-16)? When do you think that has happened, is happening, or will happen?

4. What's significant about God's kingdom according to Colossians 1:9-14?

5. What do you think are the differences or similarities between the explanations of the kingdom you've read so far?

SESSION 11: KINGDOM LIFE
WHICH KINGDOM IS WHICH?
LEADER'S SMALL-GROUP WORKSHEET

1. What are some of the major components of a kingdom?
   Possible responses: People, land, food/water, leadership, laws.

2. What is God's kingdom according to 1 Chronicles 29:11? How long does it last (Psalm 145:13)?
   Possible response: God's kingdom is all things, and his kingdom lasts (rules) forever.

3. What's the kingdom like that God has promised to set up here on earth (2 Samuel 7:12-16)? When do you think that has happened, is happening, or will happen?
   Possible responses: It's set up through David's offspring and lasts forever. Some might say it hasn't happened yet (it's coming when Jesus returns). Some might suggest Jesus is ruling now as David's heir and the kingdom is more spiritual than physical.

4. What's significant about God's kingdom according to Colossians 1:9-14?
   We are part of this kingdom.

5. What do you think are the differences or similarities between the explanations of the kingdom you've read so far?
   There seem to be differences in times, places, and even the people involved. They all show commonality in the fact that God is ruling.

KNOWING YOUR FATHER

OVERVIEW

The purpose of this lesson is to take students to the next level of their knowledge of God. Students will examine where they are with God on a personal level, understand what it means for God to be their Father, and begin developing an open relationship with their heavenly Father.

SETTING THE TONE

If you've grown up without a father, then the concept of God as your heavenly Father can be a difficult one to grasp. God's references to himself as "Father" don't always conjure up a pleasant image for people. Author Donald Miller grew up without a father, and he then struggled with the image of God as his heavenly Father. But he eventually came to an interesting place. This is what he has to say in *To Own a Dragon: Reflections on Growing Up Without a Father:*

> After all, the metaphors—love between a father and a son, between a man and a woman—didn't have to be exact. They were only supposed to make a motion, to *grunt* toward the inexplicable. And we don't *all* get to experience *all* the metaphors. A person who never leaves China doesn't get to appreciate God's handiwork in Yosemite National Park, but he will have his own versions there in China. This was important to me, because it meant that, even though I didn't have a dad, I still knew about love, and from plenty of places. So, while all the metaphors weren't firing, some of them were. I could still understand God was loving and kind, because I knew about love and kindness. And I could still understand Him as the Father to the fatherless, even if not firsthand.

I experienced this as well, and my story is all too common. At 15 I felt abandoned by my father when my parents divorced and he moved out. I began to gravitate toward anyone who could be a father figure for me. My youth pastor, my grandfather, and other men seemed to fill the earthly need pretty well. But only as I came to understand God as my Father who says, "Never will I leave you; never will I forsake you" (Hebrews 13:5), did I find a real peace. And you know, the better I understood my heavenly Father, the more I desired to have a right relationship with my earthly father.

My father and I have a good relationship now, but that never would have happened if my youth pastor had simply preached to me about honoring my parents in the midst of my struggle. You see, that was merely an outward struggle.

Instead, my youth pastor—and others like him—encouraged me to get to know my never-failing Father better. And from this newly developed relationship with God sprung a desire for me to honor my earthly parents, regardless of their mistakes.

Your students can also begin to understand God as their Father regardless of their past experiences and in spite of their current relationship with him. Some students may have really connected with one or more of the previous metaphors—God as Person, Spirit, Love, or King. Perhaps this one, though, will reach down into the hearts of some of your students and help them come to meet God as *their* Father.

BREAKING THE ICE
(7-10 MINUTES)

YOU'LL NEED

• A copy of the "Crayon" video from Highway Video (*Vibe Video Vol. 11*) and a way to show it

(Note: Either of the optional activities in today's "Breaking the Ice" section will serve as a review for what students have learned so far through this study.)

OPTION 1: CRAYON

Start your session by playing the video "Crayon." It provides a great review of the concepts you've covered to this point, and it also ends on a note about "Dad."

QUESTIONS TO ASK

1. **What concepts that we've already discussed about God did you see in that video?**
2. **Which of those descriptions of God has meant the most to you?**
3. **How did the video end?**

YOU'LL NEED

- Kids' craft materials (crayons, watercolors, scissors, construction paper, glue, and so on)
- A "Dad" or "Father" themed craft project, prepared in advance or during the activity

OPTION 2: CREATE LIKE A KID

Set out a variety of kids' craft materials such as crayons, watercolors, scissors, construction paper, glue, and so on. Ask your students to think back to when they were kids and recall the types of crafts they liked to do. Encourage them to use the provided craft supplies and make anything they want—as long as it represents something they've learned about God during this study. You may want to review with them the overall topics of the past sessions to get them thinking.

In advance, or while students are working, create a craft of your own that includes the word *Dad* or *Father.* When students are done, have a few of them share their creations with everyone.

QUESTIONS TO ASK

1. **What concepts that we've already discussed about God are represented in your creation?**
2. **Which of those descriptions of God has meant the most to you?**

Show your craft project to the students and tell them it represents a description of God you'll be talking about today—God as their heavenly Father.

TRANSITIONAL TRUTH

In his book *Knowing God,* renowned theologian J. I. Packer says, "The revelation to the believer that God is his Father is in a sense the climax of the Bible, just as it was a final step in the revelatory process which the Bible records."

If God really created the world, it doesn't necessarily mean something to us personally. God as King doesn't bring us much closer to God than we are to the president of the United States. God as a Father, though—that's personal. You might struggle with the concept of God as a Father because of previous experiences in your family. But keep an open heart and mind throughout this session, and I believe you'll feel differently about it in the end. In order to help us with this description, let's take a look at what we think of when we hear the word *father*.

SHARING YOUR PERSPECTIVE—PART 1
(7-8 MINUTES)

YOU'LL NEED
• Clay or Play-Doh

CLAY FATHERS

Give the students clay or Play-Doh to create an image of a father. Say something like—

> Take the clay and mold it into an image of what you think a father is. Be honest and real. Not everyone gets warm fuzzy feelings about their dad. You can make more than one image if it will help your illustration, but be prepared to explain your models to the rest of the group.

QUESTIONS TO ASK

1. How does your view of what a father is affect the way you view God?
2. If you created a general model of a father (not of your dad), how does your personal relationship, or lack thereof, with your earthly father affect how you view God as a Father?

TRANSITIONAL TRUTH

We all have different perspectives on fathers, and none of them are right or wrong. It's just how we feel based upon our personal experiences. But our experiences always have to be balanced by something concrete—a standard. God is the "daddy standard." Whether or not our earthly fathers come close to God's standard doesn't change who God is. The God we've been studying is above all. "For us there is but one God, the Father, from whom all things came and for whom we live" (1 Corinthians 8:6).

It is God the Father who is described in 1 Peter 1:3-4: "In his great mercy he has given us new birth into a living hope through the resurrection of Jesus Christ from the dead, and into an inheritance that can never perish, spoil or fade. This inheritance is kept in heaven for you."

Ephesians 1:4-5 also speaks of the Father, saying, "In love he predestined us for adoption to sonship through Jesus Christ, in accordance with his pleasure and will."

God chooses, according to his mysterious will, to love us. But God doesn't do this from a distance. God desires closeness—as a father with a child. God adopts us. Let's look at God's letter to us to learn more about this relationship and what it means.

YOU'LL NEED

- Copies of the **It's All About Relationship** worksheet, one for each smaller group of students
- Pencils
- Bibles

HEARING THE WORD
(8-10 MINUTES)

IT'S ALL ABOUT RELATIONSHIP

Have the students get into small groups and hand each one a copy of the **It's All About Relationship** worksheet found on **page 141**. Give the groups time to answer the questions.

When most are finished, have each group share a couple of their answers with everyone.

TRANSITIONAL TRUTH

Strike that, reverse it—"He was in the world, and though the world was made through him, the world did not recognize him. He came to that which was his own, but his own did not receive him. Yet to all who did receive him, to those who believed in his name, he gave the right to become children of God—children born not of natural descent, nor of human decision or a husband's will, but born of God" (John 1:10-13).

In his book *Knowing God*, J. I. Packer emphasizes that our relationship to God as Father is so crucial by saying, "The entire Christian life has to be understood in terms of it." If we truly know and understand God as our Father and allow his love to take us in, then everything changes.

SHARING YOUR PERSPECTIVE—PART 2
(6-7 MINUTES)

WHEN LOVE TAKES YOU IN

Say something like—

> Adoption is a miraculous process. Whether a child is orphaned because of an accident or illness, or because the birth parents, for whatever reason, can't keep and care for the

YOU'LL NEED

• A copy of the "When Love Takes You In" music video by Steven Curtis Chapman (available on YouTube) and a way to show it child, the result is the same—a child is in need of loving parents. Adoption is the process by which a couple who determines to care for that child can then be given the right to become the child's parents. This child isn't naturally born to the parents but is a child by the will (or desire and choice) of the adoptive parents. The same is true of God's relationship with us. It's only by God's desire and choice that we become his children, and our lives can change as a result.

Christian recording artist Steven Curtis Chapman has experienced firsthand the powerful change that adoption brings. Reflecting on that change, Chapman writes, "Everything changed for the Chapman family when they decided to adopt, but no one's life changed as much as the child who was adopted."

As we watch this video about the Chapmans' experience with adoption, consider how their story compares with what God wants for you.

Play the video "When Loves Takes You In" by Steven Curtis Chapman. (This video is available numerous places on the Internet, including the Web site www.shaohannahshope.org, where you can learn more about the Chapman family's adoptions, as well as request their "Building a Bridge of H.O.P.E." resource guide. The music video "When Love Takes You In" is on the included DVD.)

TRANSITIONAL TRUTH

Has your mom ever said, "Ask your father," when you've asked her for something? Well, when it comes to your heavenly Father, that's good advice. You might have some really serious needs that you want someone to meet. Rather than chasing after solutions, why not do what Jesus suggests in Matthew 7:7-11:

> "Ask and it will be given to you; seek and you will find; knock and the door will be opened to you. For everyone who asks receives; those who seek find; and to those who knock, the door will be opened. Which of you, if your son asks for bread, will give him a stone? Or if he asks for a fish, will give him a snake? If you, then, though you are evil, know how to give good gifts to your children, how much more will your Father in heaven give good gifts to those who ask him!"

MAKING IT PERSONAL
(9-10 MINUTES)

ASK YOUR FATHER

Pass out some nice stationery, pens, and envelopes to each student. Ask them to write their name and address on the front of the envelope. Then let them know that in a few weeks they'll receive the letters they're about to write as a reminder of your time together. No one else will see the contents of the letter because they'll seal their envelopes before they hand them to you. All you'll do is put stamps on them and stick them in the mailbox.

YOU'LL NEED
- Stationery
- Pens
- Envelopes

Say something like—

> **Take some time to write a letter to your heavenly Father. Ask him for whatever it is that you need. Do you need to be adopted? Do you need some advice for a situation you're in or a decision you're making? Do you need some help with family issues? Whatever it is, ask your Father for it believing that God will respond. Take seven to eight minutes to write, then silently read your letter as a prayer to God. When you've finished, seal your letter in the envelope and leave it with me.**

BRINGING IT TOGETHER

As the students turn in their letters, give each student a copy of the **Adoption Certificate** from **page 143.** They can fill it out personally and keep the certificate in their Bibles or another place where they'll see it regularly—a reminder ... they belong to their heavenly Father. Make a personal connection as you give each student a certificate. And let all your students know that you hope this study has challenged them to take the next step in their relationship with God. Tell them you're willing to be a witness for them anytime they're ready to fill out their certificate.

SESSION 12: KNOWING YOUR FATHER

IT'S ALL ABOUT RELATIONSHIP
SMALL-GROUP WORKSHEET

If God has adopted us, then…

1. What's our relationship to Jesus? (John 20:17-18; Hebrews 2:11-13)

2. What's our relationship to Creator God? (Galatians 4:4-7)

3. How should we respond to this new relationship? (1 John 3:1-3)

4. How does our relationship with those around us change? (1 John 4:7-12)

5. How does your life resemble that of a son or daughter of God?

SESSION 12: KNOWING YOUR FATHER
IT'S ALL ABOUT RELATIONSHIP
LEADER'S SMALL-GROUP WORKSHEET

If God has adopted us, then...

1. What's our relationship to Jesus? (John 20:17-18; Hebrews 2:11-13)
   Jesus is a brother to us. There seems to be a reference that we're also his "children."

2. What's our relationship to Creator God? (Galatians 4:4-7)
   We are God's sons (and daughters).

3. How should we respond to this new relationship? (1 John 3:1-3)
   Possible response: We should be living like we're part of the family—in purity.

4. How does our relationship with those around us change? (1 John 4:7-12)
   Possible response: We are to love one another with the love of God.

5. How does your life resemble that of a son or daughter of God?
   Your students may also come up with ways their lives don't resemble God. Talk about why this is and what they might do to change it.

KNOWING YOUR FATHER 143

ADOPTION CERTIFICATE

Dear friends, now we are children of God, and what we will be has not yet been made known. But we know that when Christ appears, we shall be like him, for we shall see him as he is. All who have this hope in him purify themselves, just as he is pure.

1 JOHN 3:2-3

THIS CERTIFIES THAT

DATE

WHO WAS BORN INTO FALLEN HUMANITY ON

WAS ADOPTED BY   **GOD THE FATHER**

SIGNATURE OF ADOPTING PARTY   *Jesus Christ*

SIGNATURE OF WITNESS   EXPIRES   **NEVER**

From *Creative Bible Lessons in Essential Theology* by Andrew Hedges. Permission to reproduce this page granted only for use in buyer's youth group. Copyright © 2009 by Youth Specialties.